THE WORLD'S MOST ELECTRIFYING ROCK 'N' ROLL BAND!

AC/DC

THE KERRANG! FILES!

The definitive history edited by Malcolm Dome

Virgin

First published in 1995 by
Virgin Books
an imprint of Virgin Publishing Ltd
332 Ladbroke Grove
London W10 5AH

A catalogue for this book is available from the British Library.

ISBN 0 86369 908 1

DESIGN: Jason Taylor

CONTRIBUTING WRITERS: Geoff Banks, Dante Bonutto, Steffan
Chirazi, Paul Elliott, Murray Engleheart, Steve Gett, Howard Johnson,
Don Kaye, Dave Lewis, Pete Makowski, Steve Mascord, Derek Oliver,
Mark Putterford, Ian Ravendale, Dave Reynolds, Xavier Russell,
Sylvie Simmons, Phil Sutcliffe, Mick Wall, Chris Watts, Chris Welch,
Ray Zell

PHOTOS: Dick Barnatt, Fin Costello, Erica Echenberg, Gems, Mick
Hutson, Bob King, Lorne Resnick, Ebet Roberts

PRODUCTION EDITORS: Clare Dowse (*Kerrang!*),
Gill Woolcott (Virgin)

ACKNOWLEDGEMENTS: Phil Alexander, Geoff Barton, Paul
Forty, Paul Harries, Dave Henderson, Val Janes, Dave Mustaine, Mal
Peachey, Redferns Pictures, Paul Rees, Vince Scriver, Sharon Taylor

TYPESET BY: *Kerrang!*

REPRO BY: Rival Colour Ltd, London E14 9RL

Printed and bound in Great Britain by Butler & Tanner Ltd,
Frome and London

EDITOR'S EXCUSES

❝ "I could say something deep and meaningful at this juncture, and waffle on endlessly – as indeed, I am quite capable of doing – about the legend that is AC/DC. But, well, it just seems like a complete waste of time and effort on my part. If you don't like Acca Dacca, then what the hell are you doing with this book in your hands?!

No, you're a fan of the band already, so, you don't need any encouragement to delve into the printed page and gain the most complete insight yet into the mind and spirit of the Aussie boys – says he, blowing his own trumpet!

What we've done here is to use the extensive and unique *Kerrang!* files to provide a documentary on the band's history. Hell, we've even gone back into pre-history when *Kerrang!* wasn't even a twinkle in a publisher's eye! And in order to get the early years straight, we've used the weekly magazine that spawned the mighty *K!*, the now sadly defunct *Sounds*, as a reference point.

Hopefully, the final product will give you a good laugh in places, as well as bring back some fond memories and perhaps factually surprise you at certain points. In short, it's the sort of book that once you pick up you won't want to put down – yep, we've covered the book in superglue!

I'd like to say it's been fun to put this book together, but it's been a matter of blood, sweat and tears – well, a bit of toil anyway! No, the fun comes now, knowing that we've produced a book that will bring joy and happiness to AC/DC fans everywhere. And if you believe that load of old flannel..." **❞**

'MAD' MALCOLM DOME

CONTENTS

INTRODUCTION BY DAVE MUSTAINE

CHAPTER ONE: DRUMS, GEETARS, LIGHTS – ACTION
The early days, before the formation of the band.

CHAPTER TWO: A LI'L SHOCK TREATMENT
The formative years of the band in Australia and the recording of the first albums.

CHAPTER THREE: DIRTY PROMISES
The relocation to the UK, 1976.

CHAPTER FOUR: AND THE GEETAR MAN PLAYED GEETAR
The 'Let There Be Rock' era, 1977.

CHAPTER FIVE: HELLO AAAMERICAHHH!
AC/DC conquer the States, 1977.

CHAPTER SIX: A COMING OF AGE
The 'Powerage' era, 1978.

CHAPTER SEVEN: ALL HELL BREAKIN' LOOSE
The 'Highway To Hell' era, 1979-80, and the introduction of producer Mutt Lange.

CHAPTER EIGHT: DEATH OF A SUPREME SALESMAN
The death of Bon Scott, 1980.

CHAPTER NINE: FEEL THE BLACK WIND
The introduction of Brian Johnson and recording of 'Back In Black', 1980.

CHAPTER TEN: WE, MONSTERS!
The Donington appearances, 1981/1984/1991.

CHAPTER ELEVEN: CANNON FODDER
The 'For Those About To Rock' era, 1981-83.

CHAPTER TWELVE: SWITCHED ON, FIRED UP!
The 'Flick Of The Switch' era: the departure of drummer Phil Rudd, 1983/84.

CHAPTER THIRTEEN: FLYING IN OVERDRIVE
The 'Fly On The Wall'/'Who Made Who' era, 1985.

CHAPTER FOURTEEN: THE ALL-ELECTRIC BLOW-JOB!
The 'Blow Up Your Video' era, 1988-90.

CHAPTER FIFTEEN: ON THE CUTTING EDGE
The 'Razor's Edge' era, the replacement of drummer Simon Wright, 1990-93.

CHAPTER SIXTEEN: GOING LIVE... AND BEYOND!
Bringing the story up to date.

DISCOGRAPHY: LET THERE BE ROCK
AC/DC's Rock legacy detailed.

INTRODUCTION

The year is 2000, you've just bought a guitar, dropped a few plutonium pellets into it and you choose from your sound selector switches. Yes, there it is – that sound. The Gibson SG/Marshall amplifier sound that those guys from Australia made famous. Huh?

'Those guys from Australia' are the world-famous band with the li'l kid in his school uniform, right? The kid who does a strip show during 'Bad Boy Boogie', right? The kid named Angus, right?

Who are we trying to kid? *This* is AC/DC. I can still remember the first time that I heard them.

My first record was 'Let There Be Rock' – kinda fitting for my Metal baptisim, I thought. I'd just got back from a music store that a friend had worked at, and I just liked the cover. I sat back, did the usual things to get in the mood: bolted the door, battened down the hatches, drew the curtains and dropped the needle onto the turntable.

HELLO! What the hell just happened?!

That was the day that AC/DC changed my life forever. From the first time I heard them, I knew that I had to get everything that they ever put out. From the first crackle of needle touching vinyl, till I had to try and stand up to flip the disc, till the smoke cleared, I knew someone was singing my song.

I was too blown away to really figure out what was happening until about the third song, not that 'Go Down' and 'Dog Eat Dog' didn't do anything for me. Lord knows, I was too busy putting my eyes back in the proper sockets before I figured out that these guys were for real, and that I might finally dare to set another record over in the sacred spot I'd saved for my Led Zeppelin records.

By the time I'd gotten to 'Overdose' I started to make out the words because of the accent of the singer. But it was with 'Let There Be Rock' itself that I was christened in the purest form of headbanging bliss I had ever experienced. And then it hit me. Besides wishing to one day meet them, I would love to be like them. I wanted to play like them... I wanted to sound like them... I wanted to sing like them.

Unfortunately the closest I've ever come to meeting one of the most influential bands in the turning point of my life was doing an interview for Ray Coke's 'MTV's Most Wanted' show, on the same show that Angus did a telephone interview.

For anyone who has never heard AC/DC, welcome to the planet. For all the others who shared my same experience... wasn't it great that someone was finally singing our song?

R.I.P. Bon. 'Back In Black' was a fitting tribute. I think he'd be proud of what AC/DC have gone on to achieve.

DAVE MUSTAINE, MEGADETH

sounds **HEAVY METAL SPECIAL**

No.1 June 1981 50p

KERRANG!

featuring
the
official
All-Time
HM
Top
100!

In colour . . .
**MOTORHEAD!
GIRLSCHOOL!
UFO! SAXON!
KISS! TRUST!
SCHENKER!
WILD HORSES!
PAT BENATAR! Z Z TOP!
STYX! VARDIS! TED NUGENT!
BLACKFOOT! GRAHAM BONNET!
 NIE MONTROSE! ROSE TATTOO!**

7

This book is respectfully dedicated to AC/DC fans the world over, and to the memory of the late, great Bon Scott...

CHAPTER ONE

DRUMS, GEETARS, LIGHTS – ACTION!

"Do I like AC/DC? Of course I do! I think I liked the fact that Angus definitely turned people on to wearing knickers in the US. You know, they were mechanical music at its best – and I mean that completely in a complimentary sense. Because AC/DC added everything to a party. I mean, if there was a fight at your party, you just put 'For Those About To Rock' on the stereo, turned it right up and it just took its own course!"
– Shannon Hoon (Blind Melon)

Everybody loves AC/DC. They're an institution. Rather like the 'Dad's Army' TV series or Henry Cooper or seaside postcards, you can't help but have an affection for them. There might be more successful bands. Hell, there are probably bands who have a more fanatical following, but AC/DC are out on their own. Life without Acca Dacca isn't worth even contemplating.

There is something reassuringly ordinary about the band that makes them almost the quintessentially English Rock act: Brian Johnson's ever-present cloth cap, Angus' rather fetching schoolboy outfit, the incredible whirlpools of sweat they generate each and every time they take to the stage. The amazing thing is that for most people AC/DC are, and will always be, 'that Aussie band who made rather good'!

Pretensions are as alien to this lot as beer is to a teetotaller. For AC/DC, jeans and T-shirts are all the 'props' they need (instruments aside) before setting out to rock the many thousands of fans who turn up each and every night of a world tour. Sure, there's the hardy-perennial cannons and the 'Hell's Bell', but the Young brothers (Angus and Malcolm) and their troops are about music rather than style, presentation rather than dressing.

Their music was always – will always be – supremely testosterone-friendly. But it's never been the sole province of the male Metal maverick. You can take your girlfriend to one of their gigs, in the full and certain knowledge that she'd at least enjoy the experience. There might be sexism in the lyricism, but it was 'Carry On' in outlook and attitude. There are always smiles on their faces.

AC/DC: just five ordinary blokes who turn up for work, get out of their jeans and T-shirts, step into their jeans and T-shirts – and rock the globe.

I remember seeing 'em for the first time at The Red Cow in Hammersmith, a pub small enough to fit several hundred times or more into the sort of arenas that are now their province. I saw them on that occasion almost by accident – and not many others on that night seemed to have encountered the same accident. It wasn't packed by any means, but the energy, the power, the music, the passion – that was undeniable. Already certain traits were there: Angus' ramshackle school uniform and rather cumbersome satchel, Bon Scott's bare-chested barrowboy bonhomie, the sheer groove of their songs and that will to succeed.

Years later, nothing much has changed – except they've bought Angus a nicer uniform to wear. Bon has gone, to be replaced by the Geordie brassiness of 'Johnner' Johnson, and the stages are a little bigger. AC/DC, though, still remain the biggest Pub Rock band there is – and that's the highest compliment I can pay!

They didn't start at the top. They didn't even start at the Red Cow (always thought it was something of a strange name). No, history dawned for AC/DC back in the early '50s. So, come with me on a journey back to Scotland.

Malcolm Young was born on January 6, 1953 into a large Scottish working class family. He was the sixth child for the Young clan, who were living in a modest Glasgow house and struggling to make ends meet. And when yet another child arrived on March 31, 1955, christened Angus McKinnon (a very Scots name!), the family decided that the struggle of everyday life in the harsh environs of Glasgow was no longer something they wished to endure. The pain and hardship simply wasn't getting them anywhere. So, in 1963 (the year of the big Winter freeze in the UK), the family emigrated to the sunnier climes of Australia. To be precise, they settled in Sydney, New South Wales, one of the country's premier cities and a place alive with opportunity for all. It really was, to the Youngs, the land of hope and dreams.

By this time, one Young sibling had already dabbled a little with music, although nothing particularly grandiose. Alex played the trombone and saxophone and was subsequently to pursue a professional career under the name of 'George Alexander'. And brother George, who was 17 by the time the family relocated to Australia, was to be the first member of the clan to take the plunge into the world of rock 'n' roll.

George had shown some prowess as a footballer back in Scotland, but this never amounted to enough to make him pursue any sporting ambition – Dennis Law he was not. So, he elected instead to don a guitar and carve out a name for himself as something of a minor music celebrity.

When the Young family moved to Sydney, George fell in with an number of teenagers who shared the fascination with the way in which The Beatles were then starting to reshape the music scene. At the time, the Liverpool foursome were inspiring countless aspiring musos to form beat combos of their own and strike out on the path to fame, fortune and sexual conquest.

Most, of course, would fail. But George wasn't among 'em. Thus were formed The Easybeats. George was on guitar, together with 'Little' Stevie Wright on vocals, Dick Diamonde on bass, Gordon Fleet on drums and Harry Vanda (going under the stage name of Harry Wandan) on guitar.

The quintet quickly made their mark on the Sydney scene. Their sound was sufficiently similar to The Beatles' to attract the local youth, but they could deliver with a certain individuality and flair that made them stand out from all the wannabes. They got themselves a residency at the Beatle Village Club in Sydney (the name says it all), and in 1964 landed a deal with Parlophone in Australia. The man who signed 'em to the label was one Ted Albert, who was to play (alongside George Young and Harry Vanda) a significant role in the forma-

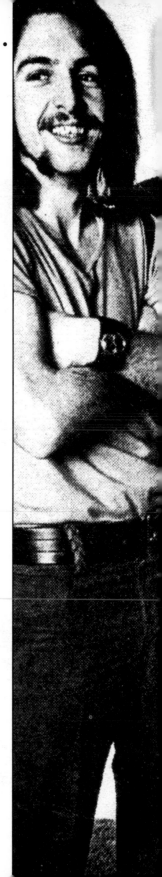

tive years of AC/DC.

The Easybeats were to become Australia's biggest Pop act during the mid-'60s, enjoying no less than five hits – a run that began with the chart-topping 'She's So Fine' in 1965. But the local scene was very parochial. Being 'big in Australia' didn't mean much in global terms. So in 1966 the band headed to the UK, to take on the big Pop guns in their own backyard. And, despite all the competition, The Easybeats quickly established themselves in Britain thanks to the fondly-remembered 'Friday On My Mind', a Top 10 hit and a song that has become something of a minor classic during the past 30 years, with the likes of David Bowie and Gary Moore covering the song.

However, by the end of the decade The Easybeats had beaten a path to inevitable obscurity. Vanda and Young returned to Sydney to work for Ted Albert in his newly formed Albert Productions organisation. But the success of The Easybeats was to have an enormous impact on the fledgling Malcolm and Angus – especially when, at the height of what was quaintly termed 'Easyfever', the family home was invaded by a veritable throng of young girls, who had discovered George's address through the local media!

The fact that George seemed to easily attract adoring females just because he strummed a guitar got his two brothers thinking. And led them into taking action...

Malcolm was the first to make tentative moves towards playing the guitar. With ad hoc advice along the way from George he made rapid

THE VELVET UNDERGROUND (WITH MALCOLM YOUNG, SEATED): DEFINITELY NOT A BAND WHO WALKED ON THE WILD SIDE!

progress, although this wasn't exactly appreciated at his school, Ashfield Boys High School, where his connections with The Easybeats and his feisty, fighting nature made him a natural target for authority. And this reputation rubbed off on Angus, when he started at the same school two years after Malcolm.

"I was caned on the first day just to make sure I didn't get any of his ideas," he was to recall to *Sounds* years later. Maybe this was an apocryphal reminiscence, but fast-food Freuds (Sigmund rather than Clement!) everywhere might believe that Angus' subsequent school-boy stage outfits might have been his subconscious way of rebelling against his school's corporal attitude towards any guitar hero aspirations he might have harboured. Kinda hoist by your own school tie!

Of course, this action by Ashfield High didn't have the desired effect. Angus was soon plucking away merrily at any guitars lying about the house, before finally getting a model of his own (guitar, not woman – that came later on).

He was to laugh at the memory during the late '70s: "It was a cheap little acoustic."

These days, Angus could probably buy the company, let alone just one instrument!

Back then, though, he contented himself with getting cast-offs from Malcolm. Some families clothed younger members in the seconds from older siblings. The Youngs used guitars for the same purpose. Malcolm had, by this time, fled school and found gainful employment. He was a machine maintenance engineer for a bra company, the salary from which allowed him to upgrade the cup size of his guitars on a constant basis!

And then the inevitable happened: Malcolm decided it was time for him to form his own band. He went through a succession of outfits whose dreams far outstripped their garage confines, before joining a group called the Velvet Underground in 1971. Before you all go rushing into paroxysms of shock at the thought of the arch boogie rhythm guitarist working with the ultimate early '70s US drug-inspired outfit, let me point out that this Velvet Underground bore no relation to the legendary Lou Reed band. But there is coincidence worth mention about the Aussie Velvets.

The original singer in the band was called Brian Johnson. Not only

16

that, but Malcolm joined up when VU relocated to Sydney from Newcastle, New South Wales. A decade later, AC/DC were to recruit a vocalist called Brian Johnson, who came from Newcastle. Except that the latter was from Newcastle-Upon-Tyne, England. Still, it's strange that the first proper band Malcolm was involved with had a vocalist with the same name as the singer he's spent more of his professional life playing alongside than any other! Such is fate.

The Velvet Underground went through a number of line-up changes during their brief spell in the local limelight, but were never considered good enough to make any lasting impact.

When the inevitable happened and the Velvet Underground fell apart, Malcolm determined to put together a new outfit. At first, this was to be a one-guitar band, with a keyboard player being drafted in to fill out the sound. But a sudden change of heart on Malcolm's part led to his decision to get in a second guitarist to play alongside him. He turned to Angus...

By this point, the youngest of the Young family had already gone through the motions of forming his own band, Tantrum, and had become proficient as a musician through playing along to any records he could find in his brothers' expanding collections and also by jamming with Malcolm. He'd also given up school at 15 and gone to work for a soft porn magazine called *Ribald*. He wasn't doing anything especially debauched – he was employed as a printer!

However, Angus was to be a victim of the rapidly-emerging computer empires. The venerable trade he was learning was slowly being stifled by the advent of the technological age, so he jacked it in and went off to seek his fortune as a musician.

When the call came from Malcolm in early 1973 to team up in this new band, Angus accepted. He joined up with his brother, drummer Colin Burgess, who had experience in several bands that never really achieved anything of note (the most interesting of these was the George Hatcher Band, if only because they shared their name with a '70s British act that enjoyed far more success), plus bassist Larry Kneldt and vocalist David Evans.

The as-yet-unnamed outfit took note of the prevailing winds on the musical scene, going for an image that was consistent with the burgeoning Glam era as well as a boogie-related sound. They

FRATERNITY (WITH CURLY-TOPPED BON SCOTT, CENTRE): UNSUCCESSFUL BROTHERLY LOVE

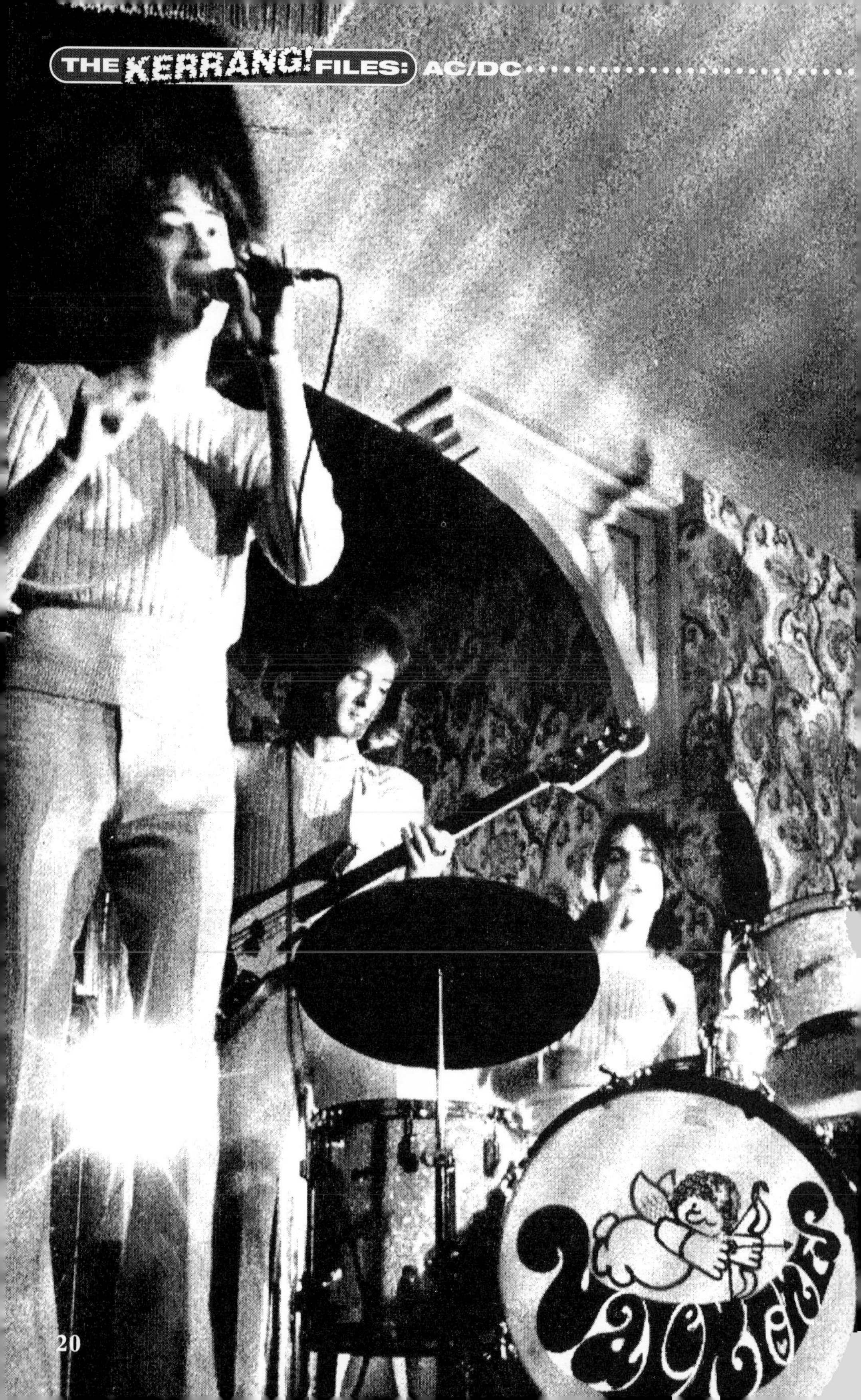

rehearsed energetically, playing cover versions and preparing to inflict themselves on an unsuspecting world. But what to call themselves?

"My sister Margaret suggested something she'd seen on the back of a vacuum cleaner: AC/DC. It had something to do with electricity," Angus told *Sounds*.

What none of the band realised was that there was also a bisexual connotation to the name, as well as that more innocent electrical reference. This fact was to haunt 'em during their formative years.

It was also Margaret who suggested to Angus that he wear a school uniform on stage. When at school, he'd dash home to pick up his guitar and slam away without bothering to change out of his uniform. Margaret believed this image could actually help him to stand out from the crowd.

On two fronts Malcolm and Angus owe much to their elder sister. Now, with a name, a sound and an image in place, all they needed was a gig. It came at the Chequers Club in Sydney on December 31, 1973. AC/DC were born, playing a covers set. The rest would be history...

THE VALENTINES WITH BON SCOTT, FAR RIGHT: RAISIN' A LITTLE HELL!

21

CHAPTER TWO

A LI'L SHOCK TREATMENT

"I'm a huge fan of the Bon Scott era. AC/DC have just written some really great songs over the years and Bon always came across to me, even on record, as someone who brought the music to life. He seemed to have so much charisma..."

- Robb Flynn (Machine Head)

In July 1974, AC/DC made their first tentative foray into the recording studio, to cut a single. The two songs involved were 'Can I Sit Next To You Girl' and 'Rockin' In The Parlour'. The recording sessions took place in June 1974 in Albert Studios, Sydney, with the team of Vanda and Young behind the production; the duo were to be hardy perennials on the production side with Acca Dacca virtually throughout the '70s.

"George produces us not because he's our brother. He thinks we're good. If we were shithouse he wouldn't do it," Angus told *Sounds* a few years later.

By the time this single was cut, AC/DC had gone through yet more line-up changes as the embryonic band tried to find their feet and focus. Drummer Colin Burgess was the first to leave, to be replaced in rapid succession by Ron Carpenter, Russell Coleman and, finally, Peter Clark. Meantime, the bass position was filled by Rob Bailey (who took over from Larry Van Knedt).

These names are worth mentioning, if only because the individuals involved were part of the extraordinary evolution of this faltering fledgling fivesome into the formidable world-class force they quickly became. The musicians may not have stuck around long enough to make an indelible mark on the band, but their place in immortality is assured merely by association.

Thus it was that Angus and Malcolm Young, Dave Evans, Rob Bailey and Peter Clark recorded that historic debut single. It was released through Albert Records in Australia during July, becoming a minor local hit; the band even got to play the A-side live on Aussie TV during this period.

AC/DC then took off on an extensive and rigorous touring schedule across Australia to augment their growing following. By this time, Angus had established his schoolboy stage presence. But in order to avoid getting verbal and physical abuse from the tough macho audiences the band usually encountered at the clubs they were booked to perform in, the diminutive guitarist would try to "come on as tough as I could.

"I'd put a cigarette in my mouth, walk onstage, stub it on the floor and hope that nobody would call my bluff!"

But that was, in a way, the least of the band's problems. There was considerably more trouble over their rather misleading name. Whilst to the young band there was nothing at all dubious about their chosen monicker, others took it to have distinct bisexual connotations – especially as this was the height of the Glam Rock era and Evans was developing a rather worrying fixation with this particular style of music, something that was to eventually lead to his musical downfall as far as Acca Dacca were concerned.

Back on the name trail, the band found themselves booked into the strangest of venues, playing at gay bars and the like before audiences who clearly believed Angus' schoolboy uniform was rather more risqué than was actually the case. The band even did a harrowing tour supporting Lou Reed at such clubs – *not* a fun time!

Still, with a single now in the shops one might have thought that matters were beginning to stabilise. However, the opposite was true. What this release and the subsequent heavy touring schedule proved to the Young siblings was that things were still not right. So they decided to relocate to Melbourne. It was here that they first hooked up with manager Michael Browning.

Browning was a local entrepreneur who owned the Hard Rock Café in Melbourne. AC/DC were booked to appear at the venue, and

AC/DC '74: THE LINE-UP RESPONSIBLE FOR THEIR FIRST SINGLE

it was here that they met Browning, who eventually took over their management affairs after saving them from a financial crisis when the band were stuck in Adelaide.

Browning proved to be a shrewd choice as manager and was to make some vital decisions for the band during the next few years. But perhaps none was to prove more important than his first – namely the hiring of a driver to ferry the band around. His name? Ronald Belford Scott, known to all and sundry as 'Bon'.

Like the Youngs, Scott was a Scot by birth, born in Kirriemuir on July 9, 1946, emigrating to Melbourne when he was six. And it was when he came to Australia that he picked up the nickname 'Bonnie', a slight corruption of the phrase 'Bonnie Scotland'. Years later, this

**THE SLEEVE FOR THE 'T.N.T.'
ALBUM, ONLY EVER
RELEASED IN AUSTRALIA**

was shortened to 'Bon' by the man himself, in order avoid the obvious effeminate tendencies of the name 'Bonnie' – and there was nothing effete about Bon!

Scott had a varied exposure to music during his formative years, learning the piano and accordion before playing both bagpipes and drums in a Scottish marching band, after he'd relocated to Fremantle, Perth in 1956. Three years later, Scott had become a fully-fledged drummer, earning numerous diplomas for his skill as a percussionist at school. He even won a youth drum championship in Perth during this period.

Never one for academic pursuits, Bon was employed as a postman whilst he attempted to break into music as a full-time career. However, the path to success was to prove rather fraught. He even ended up with a criminal record after being arrested on assault and battery charges, was turned down by the army for being socially mal-adjusted and gained a reputation for unpredictability.

His first forays into the musical world were as drummer/vocalist with bands such as The Spectors and The Valentines. The latter actually released a cover of an Easybeats song, 'My Old Man's A Groovy Old Man', in 1969 – proof of how fate can play strange tricks...

After four local hits with The Valentines, Scott left this rather

THE AUSTRALIAN 'HIGH VOLTAGE' LP

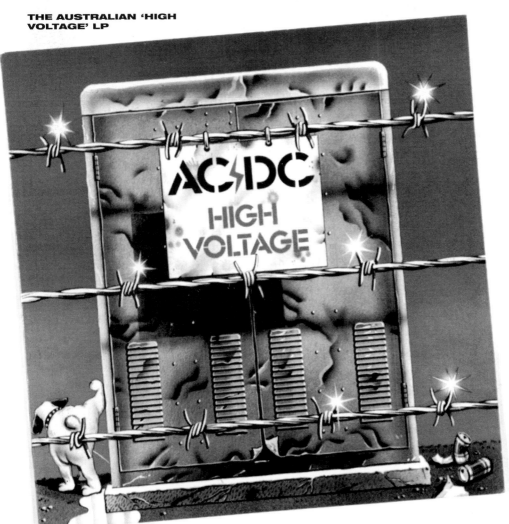

poppy outfit, moved to Sydney and joined up with Blues rockers Fraternity, wherein he augmented his drum and vocal chores with flute and harmonica.

Fraternity went on to release two albums for RCA in Australia, 'Live Stock' and 'Sweet Peach' (1971 and '72), before leaving their native shores to tour Europe. They even got to support a band called Geordie in the UK. The latter were fronted by one Brian Johnson – a remarkable coincidence!

After returning home (the European tour proved fruitless in the long run) Scott was involved in an horrendous motorbike accident that hospitalised him and ended his association with Fraternity.

Now based in Adelaide, Bon was reduced to taking on casual labouring jobs to earn a crust – and it was at this point that Browning offered him the chance to drive this 'new' band called AC/DC around. For Bon this was a golden chance to resurrect his musical career. He persuaded the Youngs to give him a chance on drums, ousting Clark in the process. And with doubts still on the horizon about Bailey, Scott was able to sneak old Fraternity mate Bruce Houwe into the line-up.

But still that wasn't enough for Scott. He harboured ambitions to front the band. He perceived that Evans' approach was at odds with Angus' and Malcolm's, on both a musical and personal level. Thus, he manoeuvred himself into position, ready to offer his services as the new frontman. And when Evans failed to turn up for a show, Scott seized his chance.

"The only rehearsal we had was just sitting around about an hour before the gig pulling out every rock 'n' roll song we knew," Angus recalled to *Sounds*. "When we got there, Bon downed two bottles of bourbon with dope, coke and speed and said, 'Right, I'm ready!'."

Bon Scott was the man who brought AC/DC into sharp focus. He was a unique personality – a man of such charisma that he could make every single fan in an audience of thousands feel like he was perform-ing just for them, whilst also having the ability to make the local pub seem like an arena. Like late comic actor Sid James, Bon was a lairy, lascivious individual, yet he transcended any accusations of sexism because of the wink in his eye and the twinkling smile on his lips. He touched everyone he met with his larger-than-life bonhomie and sense of fun. He enjoyed life and loved nothing better than giving pleasure to others. A truly gifted person, now much missed.

Yet Bon Scott was also an excessive. He couldn't turn down a drink, a blonde or a brawl – and this would ultimately lead to tragedy. Like his fellow Aussie, film actor Errol Flynn, Bon Scott simply felt he had to indulge in every aspect of life. He didn't know fear, but did have a self-deprecating streak often forgotten over the years. When Bon spoke about having 'Big Balls', it was done with a sly and knowing grin.

Without Bon Scott AC/DC might have made a major impact, but his presence certainly facilitated and lubricated their success. He was a supreme frontman and a quite magnificent interpreter of Acca Dacca's songs. Nobody could have done it better.

Now that Scott was in the band on vocals, AC/DC were ready. They holed up in a house on Lansdowne Road, Melbourne, where Bon proved to be the ultimate party marsupial. Sex 'n' drugs 'n' beer 'n' sex 'n' drugs 'n'... it was amazing the band found any time to develop their musical career. But they did. Gigging furiously, and with Bon's presence ensuring an ever-growing audience, the band had become just about Australia's biggest home-grown gigging Rock band by the end of 1974. Not that there was much competition!

Still, though, the line-up wasn't quite right. Houwe was lagging behind the rest on bass, so he was ousted and George Young came in on a temporary basis to help out his brothers. But he didn't want to relocate from Sydney to Melbourne, so the band were reduced to a foursome, with Malcolm taking over on bass. But George's influence was still there for all to see.

A deal was arranged between Albert Productions and EMI, wherein the former would record the band and then the subsequent album would come out through EMI. Effectively a production deal, it offered AC/DC full artistic control – extraordinary for a band of such limited stature.

And during the first part of '75, the band (with George on bass and one Mark Kerrante on drums) recorded their debut album, 'High Voltage', which was incredibly cut in just 10 days!

The album, recorded during any spare time the band had between gigs, came out in February 1975 in Australia. It was an immediate suc-

AC/DC '75 (FROM LEFT): PHIL RUDD, ANGUS YOUNG, MARK EVANS, MALCOLM YOUNG, BON SCOTT

cess. It opened up with the Muddy Waters standard 'Baby Please Don't Go' and contained such early stompers as 'Stick Around', 'You Ain't Got A Hold On Me', 'She's Got Balls' and 'Show Business'.

Even now, 20 years later, the unmistakable AC/DC style simply rides roughshod over the music. Vanda and Young, probably more out of necessity than anything else, kept the sound simple and rough – and it added to the growing Acca Dacca legend.

Sadly, though, it also led to Bon getting divorced. Legend has it that when his wife Irene (they got married in 1972) heard the record, it proved to be the final straw. Bon was clearly getting his lyrical inspiration to some extent from extra-marital activities – and Mrs Scott was none too pleased. They separated at this point, although the pair weren't divorced until 1978. Happily, they managed to salvage a degree of friendship from the marriage.

Two singles were quickly issued to augment the album's progress. The second of these was the number 'High Voltage', which wasn't actually on the album itself! And finally, the band found a stable line-up. In came drummer Phil Rudd, an experienced individual on the Aussie circuit, in particular with The Colored Balls, also featuring future Rose Tattoo vocalist Angry Anderson. The band released two singles, before changing their name to Buster Brown and issuing an album.

Once Rudd was recruited, he desperately needed a four-string partner. In March 1975, the band met young bassist Mark Evans when they played a date at the Station Hotel in Melbourne. Evans got involved in a scuffle with the bouncers (apparently the fracas started because he'd been previously banned from the venue for fighting) and during the ensuing *melée*, Bon and AC/DC roadie Steve McGrath jumped in to help the outnumbered Evans. They managed to persuade the hotel management not to throw the youngster out. Two weeks later, Evans joined the band – and even played one of his first shows with them at the Station Hotel

With the Young/Young/Scott/Rudd/Evans line-up now in place, the band took quantum leaps forward. And their second album, 'T.N.T.' (released towards the end of '75), clearly showed the band had made huge strides. This was something of a classic release, containing songs like 'Rocker', 'High Voltage' (finally on album), 'Live

Wire', the title track, 'It's A Long Way To The Top (If You Wanna Rock 'N' Roll)' – wherein Bon dusted down those bagpipes – and, of course, Bon's biographical 'Rock 'N' Roll Singer' and the double entendre masterpiece 'The Jack'. The 'Carry On' film team would have been proud of the last-named – nobody has ever written a more fun song about playing, er, CARDS!

The album had the trademark metronomic rhythm section, the focussed boogie guitar attack and that muscular yet quite disturbingly vulnerable vocal style. Here was a band speaking for a generation. Here was a lyricist getting onto the street, with whom teenage kids (male AND female) could readily identify. And in Australia, 'T.N.T.' was a huge success, incredibly selling more than 100,000 copies. AC/DC were the biggest thing in Aussie music – but that meant little on a worldwide level.

Thus Browning set about securing the band a worldwide deal. He landed it with Atlantic. The manager flew to London and persuaded the label managing director Phil Carson to take the band seriously (SERIOUSLY?! With a guitarist dressed as a schoolboy and a vocalist straight out the local psychiatric ward?!). Thus, AC/DC ended up with a lengthy contract with Atlantic. The reason they signed a long deal was that the company's UK arm had virtually no money to actually sign acts itself. But convinced this was a band ready to go places, Carson and his label manager Dave Dee (who had found brief Pop fame himself in the '60s band Dave Dee, Dozy, Beaky, Mick And Tich) were determined not lose them to anyone else. They therefore negotiated a contract that gave the band security of tenure for a long period – and the consequent label commitment – without having to spend vast amounts of money upfront.

Having signed the deal, Angus was flown over to London by Atlantic purely to cement relations. It was to prove a confusing, football-oriented introduction to England for the guitarist. Dave Dee virtually dragged the jet-lagged fellow off the plane and down to Stamford Bridge football ground in London to watch an FA Cup semi-final between West Ham (Dee's team) and Ipswich. West Ham won, Dee celebrated... and the teetotal Angus was left very puzzled!

Amazingly, this didn't put Angus off London at all. Far from it. And it was decided that the whole band should relocate to the UK to

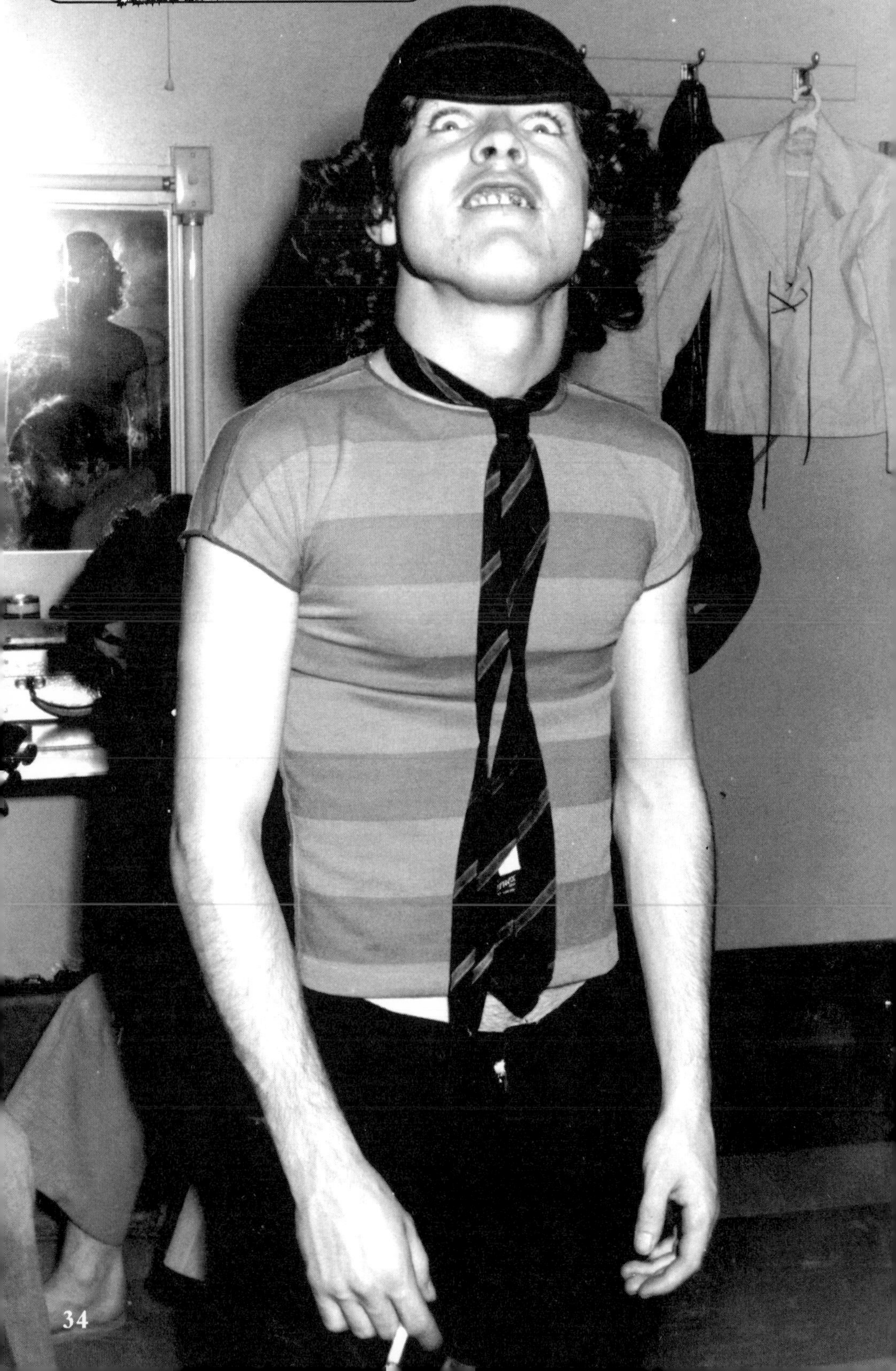

further their career. They finally landed on these shores on April 1, 1976. Leaving aside the obvious jokes about April Fool's Day, one is left to ponder whether the band were really ready to step into the cauldron that was, and still is, the UK music business after the backwoods of Australia. But, perhaps more to the point, was Britain ready for Bon Scott...?

CHAPTER THREE

DIRTY PROMISES

"Shutty is the most dyed-in-the-wool AC/DC fan in the band, but everyone was bought up on 'em really, weren't they? I'm always likely to have a compilation tape of the old AC/DC stuff in the car. Basically, they're great at what they do – the best R'n'B band in the world. They're unique..."

– Leigh Marklew (Terrorvision)

Prior to coming over to the UK, AC/DC got recording work on their third album out of the way. Once again, they were teamed with the Vanda and Young production duo. But given their incredibly tight schedule, much of the record was this time written in the studio and then put straight down on tape during a hectic two-week schedule. But at least it was now in the can, allowing the band to concentrate on live work when they finally touched down in England.

By this time the band's Aussie popularity was such that they were attracting thousands to their gigs. Indeed, a series of lunchtime shows at a well-known department store in Melbourne had to be scrapped when more than 10,000 fans turned up to the first performance. They were BIG business now down under.

But when AC/DC finally made it over to the UK, what could they expect? Limousines? Fancy hotels? Record company grovelling? Mass media hysteria? Not quite. The band went straight down to Barnes in London (close to Hammersmith), where they were ensconced in a rather dirty little house, which was to be their home for the foreseeable future.

At this point Punk was sweeping the nation. The bloated aristocrats of Rock were being swept aside. Bands such as the Sex Pistols, The Damned and The Clash were the talk of the UK music scene. Nobody, it seemed, wanted to know about the former giants of the

THE FIRST GUITAR HERO!

IN CELEBRATION of AC/DC's return to form with their current blockbustin' 'Big Gun' 45 (from the soundtrack to the 'Last Action Hero' flick), we got on the blower to our mate and 'DC mainman Angus Young to get all nostalgic! The first ever *K!* kover star took time out from writing the next AC/DC elpee and got all doe-eyed as he picked out his fave shots for the mighty *K!* and commented on them. What follows is a selection of the rarest AC/DC shots of all-time, and Angus' observations on 20 years of high voltage Rock'n'Roll as seen by Angus. Here's to the next 20, Ang!

1 "A shot of the band that goes so far back that I was still being mugged by the tooth fairy! Actually, I think we were trying to cram as many vices as possible into one photo – booze, birds, leather briefs, dirty phone calls, handcuffs, cigarettes and... er, calculators?! Well, people always told us that one day we'd have to count the cost... so we wanted to be prepared!"

2 "Another early shot. Someone once said that I was so short my legs didn't even reach the ground. I guess they were right..."

3 "This one was taken around 1976. We've always maint~~ained~~ that we aren't a 'fashion band'. Any ~~commen~~ts...?"

~~m~~akes you grow up BIG, right? I guess it just ~~goes~~ well with the cigarettes. I should point out that ~~I don't~~ stuff things down my trousers. Certainly ~~noth~~ing to, anyway..."

(page 32-33) "The shot that ended up on ~~'~~Powerage' album back in 1978. ~~ou~~r most lasting images. I suppose I look ~~a~~s tree... plenty of balls, but without the

~~by~~ Fin Costello from which some of ~~were~~ taken. As you can see from ~~where~~ we were trying to set on fire ~~(and suc~~ceeding), money in those days ~~was... ~~very tight!"

~~Famou~~s Hollywood film stars used to ~~light thousand~~s of dollars. I haven't bothered

~~and one that brings back two ~~days at school... smoking, and ~~liked~~ to wear my cap and tie a lot

~~session. Bon quite liked ~~schoolboys (check out ~~everythin~~g else you need to

~~worst nightmare – ~~with our 'Shook Me...' ~~plaintfully! Like a real ~~~~I mean (see next shot)..."

~~tying his boots in the ~~expressions. However, ~~it was nice to include a ~~~~I know he'll thank

~~of fine wines ~~about the ~~younger is ~~~~l, just pure

ANGUS CHOSE HIS FAVOURITE EVER AC/DC PHOTOS FOR *KERRANG!*, **IN JULY '93**

~~so I thought I ~~~~over the joke, ~~~~es are always

~~please)."

38

Hard Rock genre. Overnight they were classified as dinosaurs and encased in metaphorical amber, presumably never to raise their credit cards again!

AC/DC were well placed to take advantage of this change in the musical environment. They had the attitude (fights in pubs and clubs were almost *de rigeur* for them), the instinct and the music to make them instantly appealing to punks everywhere. What's more, they were for REAL. This wasn't either manufactured (like the Pistols) or bandwagon-jumping (like The Clash, who were old pub rockers). Thus, there was already a connection between punks and AC/DC.

This was accentuated by the fact that traditional Metal fans found much to applaud in the band. Atlantic were looking at a potentially HUGE act, if they played their cards right.

The band finally made their live debut in the UK during April 1976 with a series of shows at the Red Cow in Hammersmith, not far from their Barnes HQ, followed by other dates at dives and clubs around the country. They had amusingly been offered the chance to play their first show on these shores in Brighton supporting Funk-oriented band Osibisa, but had turned it down. It just wasn't right for 'em.

The early response to the band was very encouraging. They drew small yet enthusiastic audiences, with a cross-section of denim 'n' leather clad Metalheads and safety-pinned punks, who all mixed with little trouble. And although most present were unfamiliar with the material (drawn mostly from the band's first brace of albums), nonetheless Bon's costermonger charisma, Angus' frenzied fretwork (not to mention strange stage garb) and the solid-gold rhythmic propulsion allied to memorable songs, made that first tour a huge success.

Following on from this first tentative yet successful excursion, AC/DC then set out on a support tour, opening for British band Back Street Crawler. It was, on the face of it, a strange coupling. The 'Crawler had originally been put together in 1974 by Blues Rock guitar legend Paul Kossoff after his departure from Free. The band took their name from Kossoff's solo album of that title, put out in 1972. They had enjoyed modest success with the albums 'The Band Plays On' and 'Second Avenue', but weren't exactly in vogue.

However, what this tour would allow Acca Dacca to do was to

play in bigger venues under little pressure. Tragically, though, on March 19 Kossoff died from heart failure whilst flying to New York. Years of drug abuse had finally taken their toll. Yet, far from falling apart (as most expected), Back Street Crawler stayed together, shortening their name to Crawler and hiring If guitarist Geoff Whitehorn to take the place of their lost leader.

Thus, the tour went ahead. For AC/DC it was a triumph of the highest order. Everywhere the tour went, the Aussies stole the show. Their streamlined, powerhouse boogie was a revelation and the rather lumbering Crawler (bereft of their charismatic inspiration) simply could not compete. Witnessing the show at The Marquee in London for myself, it was blatantly obvious that most had turned up to see the support act. AC/DC could have comfortably headlined the tour themselves. Crawler never recovered. Neither did Acca Dacca. They were on the march, with a vengeance.

On May 14, as the tour wound towards its conclusion, Atlantic issued 'High Voltage' in the UK. Except that it wasn't really 'High Voltage', but rather a compilation of tracks from the first two albums, which drew more on 'T.N.T.' than 'HV' – rather ironic given the title!

Even the track 'T.N.T.' itself was included. Just why the album was given the 'High Voltage' monicker is anyone's guess. Perhaps Atlantic felt the title fitted the band's name more accurately.

Writing in *Kerrang!* in 1984, Mark Putterford reflected on the album thus:

THE AUSTRALIAN SLEEVE FOR 'DIRTY DEEDS DONE DIRT CHEAP'

JUNE 12, 1976 15p

Rod Stewart LP, Marley, AC/DC,
Dr. Hook, Hall & Oates, Tom Waits

so**u**nds

• **WHO**
Giant report

Would
you
give
a job
to
this
school
leaver?

See page 24

**AC/DC'S FIRST EVER
SOUNDS COVER, '76**

'The simple, infectious riff that marched in 'It's A Long Way To The Top' was the leak that would burst the banks of contemporary Rock. It introduced us bewildered Brit folk to the outrageous high voltage antics of Australia's youthful delinquents... 'High Voltage' has that brawny, rugged, street-level complexion which AC/DC were to maintain'.

With product now officially on the market and the band firmly established as a fast-rising live attraction, Atlantic knew they had a real success on their hands. How best to capitalise? Simple: trade on that school uniform look. Well, that was the label's logic.

Thus the company now teamed up with *Sounds*, regarded by then as the weekly music paper most in tune with the current Rock scene, for a low-priced tour (entrance: 50p!) that not only saw the band perform but also had videos and other goodies on offer. This 20-date trek around the country was assured massive exposure in the most vital and widely read of all the weekly music papers. By and large it proved to be a great success, although not all of the venues were sold out.

The idea behind the tour, dubbed 'Lock Up Your Daughters', was that AC/DC would be preceded onstage not by a support band, but rather a giant video screen showing a whole selection of major artists. At the time, this was an innovative approach.

The Aussie band themselves proved very popular, with Angus' regular strip show onstage a high point. And in London (at The Lyceum on July 7, 1976), this promotion between *Sounds* and the band was taken a stage further thanks to the 'Best Dressed Schoolboy/Schoolgirl' competition, compered by Radio 1 DJ John Peel. The first prize was an Epiphone Caballero guitar, won on the night by Jayne Haynes. Mind you, eyebrows were raised in certain quarters by this result – for Jayne actually worked for Atlantic!

Shortly after this tour, AC/DC were offered the chance of a weekly residency at The Marquee, every Monday beginning on July 26. It tied in nicely with the early August release of the band's new single, 'Jailbreak'/'Fling Thing' (both taken from the upcoming third album 'Dirty Deeds Done Dirt Cheap'), and helped to cement the quintet's rapidly growing stature.

The Summer of 1976 was a very hot one in the UK, especially in London. Even during mid-Winter, The Marquee (then based in

Wardour Street, Soho) could be a sweat-box. But at times during that infamous, drought-riddled Summer, it was virtually impossible to breathe. And AC/DC were packing increasing crowds into the shoe-box auditorium. They were not only breaking attendance records there, but also getting in more paying punters than the official attendance limit should have allowed.

This residency, and the band's obvious popularity, led to an offer to support Ritchie Blackmore's Rainbow in Europe during August, a three-week trek that took them to Germany, France and across Scandinavia. It was vitally important for AC/DC, as Blackmore's standing ensured that they were appearing in massive theatres and arenas, not compact clubs.

Strangely, Blackmore is supposed to have turned up at The Marquee just prior to this tour starting and is alleged to have asked whether he could jam with the band. Yet, although Acca Dacca are said to have agreed, they apparently left Blackmore tuning up by himself onstage just before this liaison was supposed to happen, having left the venue by the back door! Needless to say the famed ManInBlack (as Blackmore was affectionately known) was rather bemused by the whole affair...

The combination of Rainbow, with their roots firmly in traditional Metal, and the no-frills AC/DC seemed strange, but it worked to the latter's advantage. They returned to their English base at the end of August as a fitter, sharper and harder band, with a growing continental fan base. And on August 29 (two days after they'd appeared on TV for the first time in Britain, whilst opening for Marc Bolan at the Wimbledon Theatre in London), the band played the biggest show of their lives, appearing on the last day of the three-day Reading Festival.

Alongside the young Aussies on the bill that day were US wildman Ted Nugent, larger-than-life Southern boogie meisters Black Oak Arkansas, Jazz fusionists Brand X and smooth Pop rockers Sutherland Brothers And Quiver. It has to be said that the Oz rockers didn't quite take the day by storm, as many had predicted. Maybe it was the daylight they were forced to play in. Whatever, whilst it hadn't elevated the band's status, at least no damage had been done.

With little chance to catch their collective breath, the band (now

AC/DC ARE WELCOMED TO LONDON IN
1976 BY ATLANTIC RECORDS
A&R MAN DAVE DEE

living in a London suburb called West Brompton, which was close to the Fulham Road) were booked in to headline yet another British tour during October and November – only this time it wasn't just clubs, but a step up to theatres. It was in reality a bold, and perhaps fool-hardy, move. The band simply weren't quite ready for such a giant stride forward.

Many venues were less than half full, and some critics were begin-ning to openly wonder whether this time the band had bitten off than they could chomp. After all, they didn't have any new material to offer, Angus was still going through the same stage antics (the uni-form, the strip show, being carried around on the shoulders of Bon, who himself was stripped to the waist). Was all of it becoming just a little too stale? Had the band been over-exposed, in more ways than one?

The tour's metaphorical climax came at the Hammersmith Odeon in London on November 10 (even if the tour itself finished three days later in Newcastle). The venue's balcony wasn't even opened, and the stalls were barely half-full. But Angus lookalikes were spotted in the audience, and there was a feeling that AC/DC had become an estab-lished cult in the hearts and minds of the British youth. They had, in reality, come a long way in a short time, and whilst their audience hadn't grown with the business ambitions of the label and manage-ment, they had a foothold in Britain. And the performance at the Odeon was dazzling; they were veritable giants who had taken the step up from the pubs of April to the theatres of November in their stride.

In December, 'Dirty Deeds Done Dirt Cheap' finally appeared in the UK, three months after the Australian release and two behind the US. Missing from the British version were two tracks that had taken their place on the Aussie original, namely 'Jailbreak' (this despite its appearance as a single earlier in the year) and 'R.I.P. (Rock In Peace)'. In their stead were 'Rocker' (to be found on the original 'T.N.T.' album) and the previously unavailable 'Love At First Feel'.

But in whatever format, 'Dirty Deeds...' was a spectacular album. The title track sleazed its way into the brain, with its trademark down-home boogie beat. 'Ain't No Fun (Waiting 'Round To Be A Millionaire)' chugged along the grooves with scarcely a snarl out of

OOGIE

ROM PREVIOUZ PAGE

reduced to driving bands
d from gigs in the employ
noters. In short, Bon
ne crack:

n the highway
a show
ng on the byeways
y rock 'n' roll
robbed
ted
up
ed
ad
took
u folks
than it looks!'

ng Way To The Top
na Rock 'N' Roll'

WERE prepared for
vork. That much was
om the off, when they
ed two albums in the year

h Voltage' came first in
ary and wasn't afraid to
s roots with a cover of
standard 'Baby Please

, released in
er, really announced
DC were right down
ne gutter. The music
e mood of the
azy tales of dirty
all ages, life on the
you ain't got the
at and the adrenalin
o-frills rock 'n' roll.
y ways it could be
ed as the most
ctory three chord boogie
d ever been dreamt up.
the way AC/DC played
overdriven and far
ntense than any of the
layers from whom
olen licks, was wholly

Geor Young realised this
ch from the off and
sations that he was helping
and along purely because
ilial interest were
ssed by Angus:
rge produces us not
e's our brother. He
we're good. If we were
use, he wouldn't do it."
it seemed that the fans
tralia agreed with the
al hypothesis that AC/DC
't shithouse at all. Those
vo albums sold well
h and enabled band
Michael Browning to
ate a US and UK deal with
tic, territories where
DC would need to become
ed if their vision of
elves as a major act was
e to fruition.
band packed its
tive bags and headed for
, settling down in the
suburb of Barnes and
billed by the record
any as 'Punk Rock From
a'.

ANGUS YOUNG: 'OK, so he's paraded around in his schoolboy uniform for as long as AC/DC have been treading the boards. Somehow I can't see that that ploy was adopted to impress America's rock bimbos...'

Pic Robert Ellis

NOT THAT the climate
time made that such a
thing.
The streetwise attitude
band helped them to crea
some of the more discerni
punks whilst tours with th
likes of Back Street Craw
allowed them to introduce
themselves to the ultimate
more loyal Metal audie
The first two album we
repackaged and compre
into one dynamite parcel t
was titled 'High Voltage', a
said album was used to
introduce the band to its
market.
And, as usual, it aime
straight for the groin and
jugular in precisely that o
AC/DC have never be
about subtlety, but what ma
people have conspired to m
over the years has been the
inherent humour that Bon S
displayed in his lyrics.
'She's Got The Jack' and
I Sit Next To You Girl' are
loaded with self-deprecat
humour that should always
seen as written with tongu
planted in cheek.
Whilst Angus and Malc
piled the power on with a
frighteningly deceptive
straightforwardness, Bon w
as much a part of the band
appeal with his 'bad boy
good' bonhomie.
Basically, Bon wasn't a
say that boys will be boys
many young men (and qui
few enlightened ladies) to
the songs in the spirit wit
which they were a
Atlantic were backin
band to the hilt and in
conjunction with *Sounds*
magazine promoted the
Up Your Daughters' tour.
entrance fee of 50p and
added attraction of a sel
of hot rock 'n' roll videos
helped to ensure that the
punters were enticed t
out these Aussie scum
only someone would
kind of support into
new band these days
Of course, by the t
show came to Lond
had been hatched to
best-dressed schoolbo
schoolgirl in the audienc
the finals being judged b
Peel (!) and the girl being
the extremely honoured t
'The Schoolgirl We'd Mo
To'.
Subtlety, it seems,
one of AC/DC's stron
However, creating som
a reputation as one of th
hardest boogie bands
was, as sold out shows
tours of Europe with Ra
confirmed.

WHICH DIDN'T
that AC/DC had it
Far from it, as the band'
major hall tour of the UK
November of '76 prove
Despite the release o
was in effect the third al

place. 'There's Gonna Be Some Rockin' ' proved to be a rousing anthem, whilst 'Squealer' also had a certain bombastic personality that by this time was unmistakably AC/DC.

However, best of the lot was the trio 'Big Balls', 'Problem Child' and 'Ride On' – all bona fide classics of the '70s.

'Big Balls' celebrated Bon Scott at his most accomplished in the double entendre vein. The rhythm was groinal in origin, providing the perfect backdrop as Bon leered through the lyrics. Suffice it to say that when he spoke of his *'big ball'*, he wasn't talking about debutante coming-out parties...

'Problem Child' was virtually autobiographical in its style and content as far as Scott was concerned. Over the years it became his anthem, such was the attention to detail and the feeling among fans that this song best described the lovable, loutish lothario lyricist.

'Ride On' is one of the finest road-weary songs ever conceived. It has a depth of feeling and, yes, even loathing that opened up another side to Scott's personality. As he croons about another town, another bottle, there is a world-weary feeling. Listening back to the song from a safe distance, it's clear that Scott wasn't merely a party animal, but did have a thoughtful, even sensitive, ironic side.

Writing in *Kerrang!* some eight years after the LP first appeared, Mark Putterford was a little less enthusiastic about 'DDDDC':

'Sure, the tireless Sydney stompin' was there in force, but this time a certain sparkle was lacking. Were they treading water already...? Overall, it's not one of the band's best (albums).'

Yet, for most, the record amply showed that the band were moving ahead in leaps and bounds; they now had an instantly recognisable sound and, thanks to an incredibly extensive touring schedule, were rapidly becoming a force to be reckoned with. The next year was gonna be a crucial one...

KERRANG! MEGA METAL 16, FROM 1990

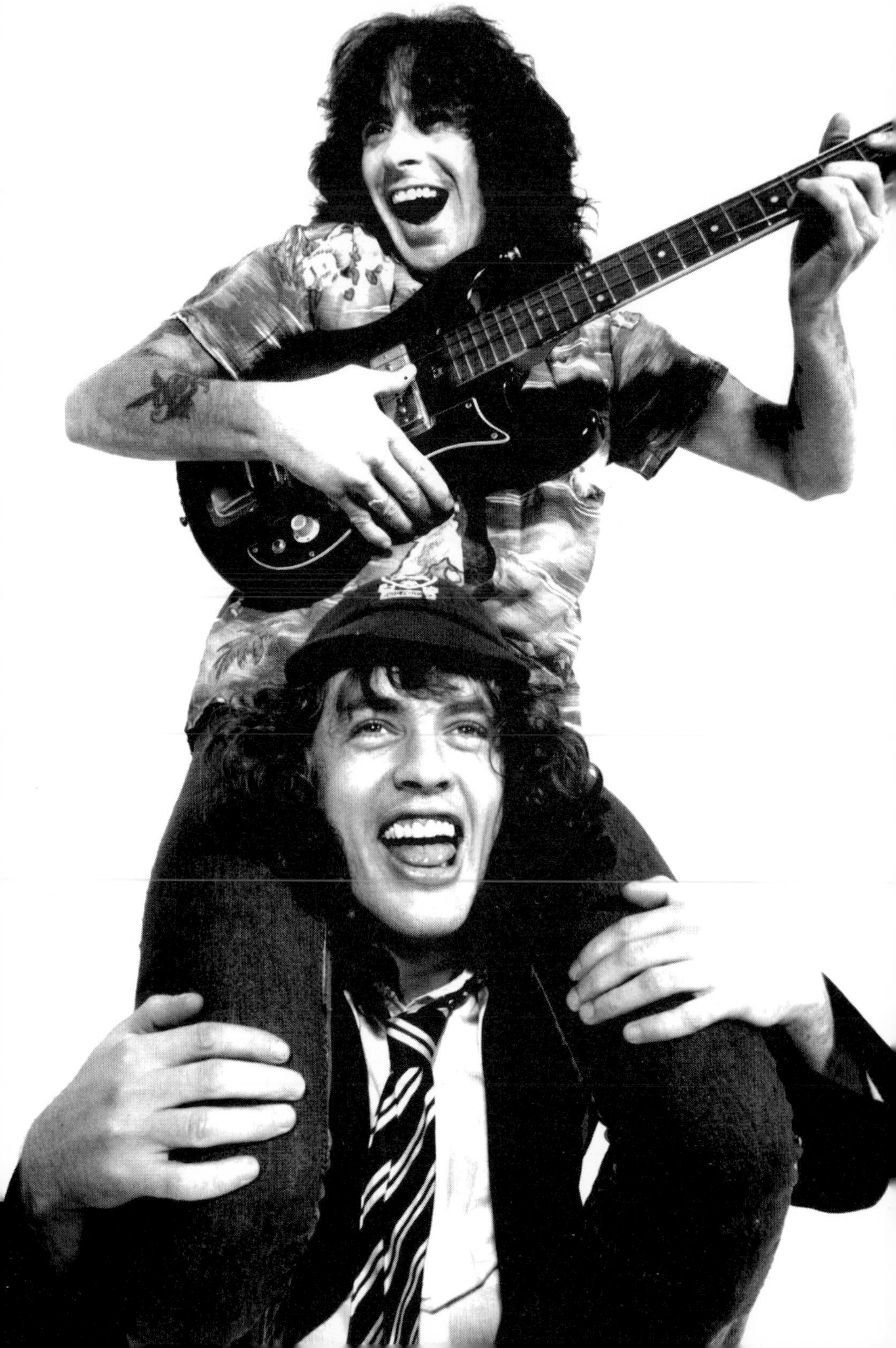

CHAPTER FOUR

AND THE GEETAR MAN PLAYED GEETAR...

"You know, when I was growing up in Canada, everyone at my school listened to AC/DC. We got high whilst playing their records. They're a band whom everyone seems to love. And everyone has done something naughty whilst listening to one of their albums..."
– David Usher (Moist)

There's an old maxim in life that you never change a winning formula. As our American friends would say: why fix it if it ain't broke? AC/DC certainly stuck to their proverbial guns for their next studio assault. Thus, back the band went to Sydney at the beginning of 1977, to work once again with the Vanda and Young production team on what was, to all intents and purposes, something of a make-or-break album for them.

Now, it may seem strange in retrospect to suggest that the band were under any pressure at the start of '77, but in fact they probably were – even if it was more below the line than blatant.

They'd conquered Australia. They'd made inroads into the UK, successfully straddling the Punk era. But could they actually sell records in sufficient quantities to really make their mark? And what of the musical Everest that was America? Was there a future for the band in the world's most lucrative record-buying market? All of these questions were now being faced, boldly and assuredly. But at the start of the year, most of us on the outside remained to be convinced that we'd been watching anything other than an excellent club/pub band who may have already reached their zenith. WRONG!

Out of the Sydney Studios came 'Let There Be Rock', an album that did more than anything before or since to elevate AC/DC into the very biggest of leagues. But it was not to see the light of day until the end of 1977. Before that, much was to happen to the band.

Touring-wise, the year began with a 26-date trek around the UK, taking in theatres and university halls. It ran from February 18 and saw AC/DC reinforcing all the ground work done in 1976. And in Edinburgh, during the second number of the set (newie 'Dog Eat Dog'), there was something of a crowd disturbance, which was quickly dubbed a full-scale riot by the media.

Given the serious controversy being fermented around the whole Punk/New Wave scene – riots, racist trouble, spitting – it certainly didn't do Acca Dacca any harm to be seen as attracting that kind of audience. It underpinned their right to be regarded in some respect as part of the new musical movement. Of course, this sort of thing did not appeal to traditional Metal fans. But the sheer forcefulness of the music seemed to overcome any peripheral fears.

Talking of 'Dog Eat Dog', the band were asked to appear on Aussie TV show 'Countdown' (the Down Under answer to our own 'Top Of The Pops'). Rather surprisingly introduced by Pop icon Leo Sayer, their performance was said to be high on the humour scale, the band (in particular Bon) taking the proverbial piss out of the whole notion of miming to their own song! Whether this was actually appreciated by the programme's producers no one seems to be certain. But AC/DC's presence on the show underscored the band's huge homeland following.

The band's next step was a major leap into the unknown, when they were confirmed as the opening act on Black Sabbath's 1977 European tour. It was an ominous prospect, but one designed to introduce them to European Metal audiences, who were (and still are) known for their abiding loyalty to any band who take their fancy.

Sabbath by this time were seen as rather old-hat, out-of-date Metal heads who should have been swept away with the advent of the New Wave. What's more, there was clearly dissent eating its way through the ranks. Ozzy Osbourne was rumoured to be very unhappy with his lot, and had apparently fallen out badly with guitarist Tony Iommi. All of which might explain why the Sabs' '77 album 'Technical Ecstasy' had been something of a commercial disaster.

So the choice of AC/DC to open for them might have been as much to bolster their fast fading glories as to give the Aussies a leg up. Result? AC/DC were declared the winners on points throughout the tour – at least, for as long as they were actually on it!

Unfortunately, an altercation occurred between bassist Geezer Butler and Malcolm Young in a hotel bar. Allegedly, the feisty Scottish Aussie punched out the hapless Sabbath bassist. A day later, AC/DC were kicked off the tour and returned to London, slightly chastened.

But this was not the end of the band's troubles. Very shortly after they came back to London, AC/DC and Mark Evans parted company. It had become obvious to all close to the band that there was a growing disenchantment between Evans and Angus that had to be tackled before it got out of hand. Thus Bon, Phil and the Young brothers met at a flat in West London where Angus and Malcolm were then living to discuss the situation – and, more importantly, the solution.

Strangely enough, it seemed that the four actually reached no real conclusion. But the writing was most assuredly on the wall. Evans' time in the band was all but up; if he didn't leave of his own volition, sooner or later he would be fired. So he jumped ship.

Subsequently, the bassist turned up in various Aussie bands, none of whom really went on to achieve anything of note. Arguably the most interesting were Heaven, managed ironically by Michael Browning and fronted by one Allan Fryer, who was considered at one time to be the hot favourite to replace Bon after his tragic death in 1980. More on Fryer a little later. The last anyone heard musically from Evans was in Los Angeles during the early '90s when he record-

A delirious delve into the AC/DC album archives by

THE EARLY DAYS (from left): Phil Rudd, Angus Young, Mark Evans, Malcolm Young, Bon Scott.

'HIGH VOLTAGE' ATLANTIC K50257 MAY '76

SNOTTY NOSTRILS a-flarin', crooked teeth a-gnashin' and grubby knees a-tremblin', the crazed Just William exaggeration begins to nod uncontrollably as his pale, boney hands jerk across the live wires in his grasp.

The simple, infectious riff that marched in 'It's A Long Way To The Top' was the leak that would burst the banks of contemporary rock. It introduced us bewildered Britfolk to the outrageous high voltage antics of Australia's youthful delinquents, AC/DC, who were destined to riff all over the opposition for years to come.

It was 1976 and the title of that 'HV' opener couldn't have been more prophetic as Blighty found herself in the throes of a spikey-haired and safety-pinned uprising. But, back in Oz, the Young brothers and their obnoxious mates Bon Scott (vocals), Phil Rudd (drums) and Mark Evans (bass) had already subjected their cowering country to a double dose of devilry in the form of 'High Voltage' and 'TNT'. A potent concoction of the two seemed the ideal arsenal (spit) to assault

GB with.

Composed of 'TNT's' entire side one, title track, 'Can I Sit Next To You' and 'High Voltage', the British 'HV' takes only 'Little Lover' and 'She's Got Balls' from its Aussie counterpart.

After the brutalism an' bagpipes of 'It's A Long Way . . .', AC/DC's own inimitable blend of relentless rock 'n' roll and humour sweeps them through 'Rock 'N' Roll Singer', 'She's Got The Jack' (for 'Jack' read 'Pox') and 'Live Wire' to great effect.

Produced by Angus and Malcolm's big brother George and his songwriting pal from his days with the Easybeats, Harry Vanda, 'High Voltage' has that brawny, rugged, street-level complexion which AC/DC were to maintain despite their rapidly rising status (and bank balance).

'DIRTY DEEDS DONE DIRT CHEAP' ATLANTIC K50323 DECEMBER '76

STARVING FOR success and bursting at the seams with crude energy, AC/DC blazed around Blighty during '76 on their 'Lock Up Your Daughters' tour which was co-promoted by Atlantic Records and *Sounds* (admission

50p!) before deliveri new album just befor Christmas.

Inside the strange which depicted sever mysterious character dog peering at us fro park of a motel, the a quite disappointing fo Sure, the tireless Sydr stompin' was there in this time a certain spar lacking. Were they tre water already?

Songs like 'Love At I 'There's Gonna Be Som Rockin'' and 'Ain't No I Waitin' Round To Be A Millionaire' tended to l down the beaten track too much flair and exci and 'Ride On' yawned p

But 'DDDDC's' savin comes from squawking Bon Scott's hilarious lyri Mostly, they were bicep Scotch-swilling and par orientated in the usual n fashion. But Scott's chee sense of humour was gr times.

'My balls are always bouncing/My balls are alwa full/And everybody cums a cums again,' he boasts duri 'Big Balls'. 'Some balls are h

24

ed an album with The Zoo, led by Fleetwood Mac drummer Mick Fleetwood.

In the meantime, as Evans headed back home, AC/DC set about the task of finding a suitable replacement. Within 24 hours of Evans telling the band that he was off, the name of Cliff Williams came to the fore. Browning had heard about him from a mutual acquaintance, and immediately made contact.

However, the rumour-mill was grinding out other names. The most ludicrous was that of former Sex Pistol Glen Matlock. Whether he was ever seriously considered or was just a joke suggestion blown out of all proportion by others remains open to conjecture, but he *was* mentioned at one point.

At least Matlock made some sort of sense (energetic bassist with an aggressive, youthful approach), but another one of the names in the frame made no sense at all: Manfred Mann's Earth Band four-stringer Colin Pattenden! His name was put forward by the Youngs, but was rejected out of hand because of his age.

Instead, Williams walked into his audition with Browning's seal of approval – and got the job. Years later, Browning admitted to *Kerrang!* and *Sounds* scribe Mark Putterford: "I tipped him off about certain things (such as using a pick and to play the songs in exactly the same way as they'd been recorded). So Cliff walks in and does everything the guys want from a bass player... Obviously, Cliff never told the band he'd been tipped off, and obviously I didn't want the band to know I'd tipped him off!"

Williams himself had a varied background. An Englishman – it made sense as AC/DC were now based over here – he was born in Romford on December 14, 1949. But he spent much of teens up in Liverpool, where the family Williams had relocated when Cliff was nine. After trying his hand at working in a factory, Williams decided to chance his arm by becoming a professional musician. As luck would have it, his first proper band, Home, featured some rather tasty musicians: guitarist Laurie Wisefield (who found fame with Wishbone Ash), keyboardsman Clive John (who went on to join Welsh rockers

KERRANG! RE-REVIEW AC/DC'S BACK CATALOGUE, 1984

53

BON AND ANGUS
GIVING IT THEIR ALL
ONSTAGE IN '77

Man) and drummer Mick Cook (who rose to prominence with Blues rockers The Groundhogs).

Williams played bass, with the line-up being completed by vocal-ist Mick Stubbs (who really went on to... very little!). Such was the interest in the style of music peddled by Home – basically, Progressive Rock with a hint of Blues – that they had little trouble lading a major recording deal with Epic in 1970. The following year, they unleashed the incredibly titled 'Pause For A Hoarse Horse' album.

Three more LPs followed – 'Home' (by which time Jim Anderson had arrived on keyboards), their one chart success 'Dreamer' (like 'Home' issued in 1972 – it reached the heights of Number 41!) and 'The Alchemist' (1973). But in truth the band never really made seri-ous commercial inroads, and when Stubbs left they became the back-ing band for folkie Al Stewart (remember 'Year Of The Cat'? Probably not...). This didn't last long, and Williams was next to jump ship, forming Bandit in 1974.

Bandit quickly got a deal with Arista and released one self-titled album in 1977. Joining the bassist in this line-up were such future luminaries as vocalist Jim Diamond (who went on to success as a solo artist) and drummer Graham Broad (who was later to join Buck's Fizz!). But 'Bandit' did little business (their basic Pub Rock style was hopelessly out of fashion), and Williams had no hesitation in jumping off his own bandwagon and into AC/DC's welcoming charabanc.

By the time that Williams had bedded himself down nicely in his new situation, the band were ready to unleash the 'Let There Be Rock' album on Britain, featuring his predecessor Mark Evans! Things were slightly out of synch still in the UK. 'Let There Be Rock' finally saw the light of day in the UK during November – and it was clear that the band had made a huge leap forward.

"George (Young) asked us what kind of album we wanted to make and we said, 'Well, it would be great if we could just make a lot of guitar riffs'. We were all fired up after doing a lot of touring," Angus told *Sounds* in '77.

The album was a star-spangled triumph from start to finish – a real quantum leap. But the whole approach was still very much LIVE – without a net. At one point it was even claimed that Angus' guitar amp caught fire in the studio whilst he was burning his way through a particularly vicious solo. A totally oblivious Angus just kept on playing for all he was worth...

Mark Putterford of *Kerrang!* was to describe this album thus: "For the first time AC/DC had a real Metal edge to their boisterous bluesy boogie, an extra heaviness which packed a fearsome kick".

And Putterford wasn't far wrong. The clear stand-out track from the vantage point of some 18 years later is 'Whole Lotta Rosie'. Voted the greatest Heavy Metal track of all time in the very first issue of *Kerrang!* in 1981, the unmistakable staccato riff that opens the whole song has become arguably the most recognisable of all Acca Dacca numbers. Live, this was to be ritualised with crowds across the world chanting Angus' name, as he delved into the opening riff. Ironic that this has become so associated with the livewire guitarist, when the story behind the song lies very much in Bon's domain.

The 'Rosie' in question was from Tasmania with the measurements of 42-39-56, as Bon intoned in the number itself! Whilst the band were out in Melbourne on an early tour, Bon was assailed by 'Rosie', who apparently strong-armed him back to her place, threw him into the bedroom... and the rest is rock 'n' roll history!

"We saw her again when we visited Tasmania," Angus told *Sounds*. "But she'd lost a lot of weight and Bon was very disappointed!"

'Rosie' took this biographical number as being something of a compliment. Moreover, Bon was far from being her only sexual conquest in a very short space of time. Indeed, he was allegedly number 29 that month! 'Whole Lotta Rosie' was typical of Bon, turning a night of soiled 'n' sordid passion into a peerless song. But then that's when Bon was at his best, taking his own experiences and making them both amusing and palatable for the masses!

Elsewhere on the album, Bon took time out to discuss personal hygiene and social disease through the aptly-titled 'Crabsody In Blue', which many saw as the sequel to 'The Jack'. Although a play on the George Gershwin Jazz masterpiece 'Rhapsody In Blue', there was actually a well-known ointment for the treatment of crabs called Blues, which made the song seem even more autobiographical. Bon was almost certainly drawing from his own experiences...

The likes of 'Bad Boy Boogie', 'Hell Ain't A Bad Place To Be' (again drawing heavily from Bon's own life), 'Dog Eat Dog', 'Go

CLIFF WILLIAMS
DURING HIS
DAYS WITH
HOME

Down' and 'Overdose' all added to the AC/DC legend, with furious, Metallised riffs taking the hitherto traditional boogie base of the band into fresh realms.

But, aside from 'Whole Lotta Rosie', it was the title track that captured the imagination. A sprawling, near epic encounter, this saw AC/DC telling the story of rock 'n' roll itself in simplistic, yet very real terms. The song, aside from having a distinctive rolling melody line, is inspired in the way in which it captures the excitement and sense of entering the unknown that surely typified the early days of Rock music.

The accompanying quasi-religious video was appropriately light-hearted, with Bon dressed up as a vicar, as the whole birth of rock 'n' roll was put into a biblical context. The whole video now seems rather primitive, but at the time was a bold step for any band to take. By the way, it was actually shot with Williams in the line-up.

'Let There Be Rock', the track, was a magnificent exposition, underlying just how AC/DC could be much more than just out-and-out guitar thrashers. The rumbling rhythms, Bon's multi-paced use of his voice, Angus' exploding lead guitar work – all of this added up to a work of near genius.

The album clearly made its mark in the UK, reaching Number 17 in a run of five weeks in the national charts. Now, they had to be taken very seriously indeed.

But by the time 'Let There Be Rock' had broken the band to a new level, they had their sights trained on America. Now, here was an even bigger challenge!

CHAPTER FIVE

HELLO, AMERICAAAHHH!

"I love AC/DC. They're the most energetic, consistent live band in the world. Angus Young is one of the best – no, THE best – performer ever!"
– Sebastian Bach (Skid Row)

For any Rock band wishing to be regarded as more than parochial paragons, America has to be the ultimate goal. The final frontier. The moment of truth. You cannot be regarded as an international success if you're not big in the States.

Thus, with Cliff Williams now firmly ensconced in the line-up, AC/DC set about the task of bringing the America to its knees. It was to prove a diverse, hectic, tiring yet rewarding time for the band. America really did take them to their heart, loving the Aussies' brash yet instant style of Boogie, Metal and Blues.

The band began their great US adventure in the Southern part of the sprawling country during the Summer, starting out in the local clubs and finding, much to their surprise and delight, that they were packing 'em in. Word had already spread, and the recent release of the 'High Voltage' album (the British version, not the original Aussie record) had clearly helped the cause.

In Florida, Acca Dacca even found themselves on the bill for an outdoor festival at the Hollywood Sportatorium before some 13,000 fans. This was a charity bash, organised to raise funds to fight muscular dystrophy. Such was the appreciation for the fivesome taking the

THE LATE, great Bon Scott. Say no more!

seasoned pro Cliff Williams, who had plenty of recording experience with the bands Home and Bandit, filled the vacant spot.

To my mind it will always be the rhythm section of Williams and Rudd that made the definitive AC/DC sound. In fact, the line-up of Angus, Malcolm, Bon, Phil and Cliff, the team which made the following three AC/DC albums, remains to my mind the definitive line-up.

There simply won't ever be another set of musicians who were so tuned into each other and to the coll...

Punk? Maybe the attitude was from the street, but musically there was no doubt that this was rock 'n' roll.

As Bon himself said: "Some reviewer said about 'Let There Be Rock' that it was sophisticated punk. But you can't have sophisticated punk on the English level of punk. This is anti-sophistication. Like, especially bad. The worse it is, the better it is." Not what AC/DC were about at all.

The band were on a roll now, with a live se... featured much of the ne... album and US...

62

time to appear, they were even given the keys to Hollywood (the Florida city, not the California silver screen playground!).

Thus, AC/DC's first jaunt across the States was a case of small clubs at one end of the spectrum (including The Waldorf in San Francisco and the Whiskey A Go Go in Los Angeles) and huge arenas at the other (supporting the likes of REO Speedwagon).

At the Whiskey, *Sounds* correspondent Sylvie Simmons described them thus: 'Onstage, cardboard cut-outs of a Heavy Metal-cum-Punk band; coupled with music, heavy, bludgeoning Rock at its most manic. Meanwhile, back in the dressing room taking it easy, the band sit with their feet up, having a drink. None of this audience-performer participation lark. No headaches or ulcers. A new generation of calm, unneurotic Rock stars.

'While record companies are dashing around snapping up anything that even smells of Punk, these beer-swilling, bad-mouthing, well, Punks seem to have been ignored in the rush. Unfazed, they have been supporting bands and headlining in clubs up and down the country. Apart from a few language problems they're having fun and winning fans'.

Sylvie acclaimed their two shows-in-one-night stint at the Whiskey to be 'a success. They were even called back for an encore'.

Amusingly, for the second show, the band were getting stuck into the backstage rider when the chant for an encore went up. So, they missed the chance!

"There's nothing worse than hanging around for an encore," Angus told Sylvie. "We always go to our dressing room. Trouble is these guys really like drinking, so as soon as they get to the dressing room they're blotto. Still trying to figure out where they are. He (Bon) thought he was in Detroit!"

"I got a letter from a girl once," Bon explained to *Sounds* at the time. "This letter said, 'Bon Scott I hate you. You're nothing but a dirty old man and you're leading this nice little Angus astray. What's he going to be like after he's been in a band with you? You're old enough to know better!'."

KERRANG! MEGA METAL 16, FROM 1990

That was typical of the way in which Angus was being perceived by the fans – the little kid – whilst Bon was the leering, sneering lothario. It wasn't doing AC/DC any harm as they crossed the States.

Arguably their finest hour or so came in New York, when they played a hectic two gigs in one night.

The band were booked to open for wild Punk-Metal gods The Dictators at The Palladium, as well as headline at the world-renowned Punk/New Wave haven CBGB's later that night! To some extent, this was a publicity stunt to get the band attention, but it was the music that was making inroads.

Livewire, stripped to the bone and a furious cocktail of sweat and emotion, the music took The Palladium by storm. Although The Dictators (led by 'Handsome' Dick Manitoba, and also featuring future Twisted Sister bassist Mark 'The Animal' Mendoza and guitarist Ross The Boss, who went on to join Manowar) were regarded as one of America's most frenetic and powerful bands at the time, they apparently couldn't live with their bone-shaking, brazen support act. AC/DC stole the honours in one of the most daring raids since the Great Train Robbery. It couldn't have been better scripted.

And Angus chose the occasion to unleash his latest weapon – a cordless guitar. The diminutive guitar hero's antics had long been held back to some extent by the length of cord he could attach to his flailing guitar. Now, at last, thanks to wonders of modern technology, he was able to free himself of such restrictions.

"It was amazing to see," Bon recalled to *Sounds*. "Angus had this Cheshire cat grin all over his face, and evil thoughts seemed to be going through his brain as to what havoc he could wreak with this evil little invention."

The band virtually came offstage at The Palladium and headed downtown to CBGB's, taking the stage before a packed audience. It was an awesome sight to behold. If any one night proved to be the turning point for them in America, then it was this one.

With the release of 'Let There Be Rock' in the wake of this live onslaught, the band had carved out a niche for themselves in the US – one that surely would see 'em ready to climb to even greater heights. America, it would seem, was at their feet – except that their record label out there was still running slightly scared of what it had before its very eyes! It has even been suggested that, were it not for the band playing at the aforementioned Hollywood Sportatorium gig, they would have been unceremoniously dumped by Atlantic in the States.

Frankly, the negative media attention the band were getting in the US from certain influential quarters (the 'Let There Be Rock' album had received something of a thumbs-down) probably had a lot to do with Atlantic's fears, not to mention the band's low-slung, low-life attitude and almost hand-me-down stage attire. In America (especially towards the end of the '70s), glitz was the buzz word. Everything literally had to be bigger, bolder, louder and brighter than everything else. Somehow, the sight of a demented school kid and a tattooed bar-room brawler leading a band who were at home in jeans and T-shirts didn't appeal to the American sensibility.

Still, the band survived, thanks in no small measure to the fact that they were more than prepared to work their balls off on the road – playing every nook, cranny and granny hole in the vast country. And towards the end of 1977, the band got yet more major breaks when they were selected to support Canadian heroes Rush and, even more importantly, the mighty Kiss, arguably the biggest live draw in America at the time.

Such was the down-market look adopted by AC/DC that they actually had trouble at more than one venue convincing security guards that they were the support act! Still, playing arenas on a regular basis was only helping to cement AC/DC's progress.

On December 7 1977, the fivesome performed a show for radio broadcast at Atlantic's own recording studios on Broadway. A special album was pressed up and sent to radio stations across the country in order to facilitate some airplay for the boys as they prepared to venture back into the studio.

So, what was the rare 'Live From The Atlantic Studios' LP like? Xavier Russell reviewed it for *Kerrang!* in 1983:

'Recorded in December '77 at the Atlantic Studios in New York, this still remains AC/DC's finest offering to date – far superior to the official live album (1978's 'If You Want Blood... You Got It'). How many copies of this gem are still floating around is hard to say, but it can't be many, as I recently saw a copy go for £40.

'The main difference between 'Live From The Atlantic Studios'

ANGUS ONSTAGE
AT AC/DC'S
LEGENDARY
PALLADIUM GIG
IN 1977

STRIKTLY FOR K[

FOR THE first time this column lives up to its name! While none of the five albums reviewed here, have been released commercially, and you're not going to see them in your high street shop, you should be able to find them in specialist stores. The Record And Tape Exchange chain occasionally carries live promos and record stalls in markets are an obvious place to check out. Happy hunting, and don't forget to scrounge a couple of extra quid off mum, as this type of record doesn't come cheap.

AC/DC
'Live From The Atlantic Studios'
(LAAS 001)
Recorded in December '77 at the Atlantic Studios in New York, this still remains AC/DC's finest offering to date – far superior to the official live album. How many copies of this gem are still floating around is hard to say, but it can't be many as I recently saw a copy go for £40.

The main difference between 'Live From The Atlantic Stufios' and 'If You Want Blood' is Bon Scott. He'd obviously had a few beers before recording 'LFTAS' and the audience being distinctly on the small side, around 50 or so crammed into the studio, this is very much a trip down memory lane (remember when AC/DC used to play the Red Cow?) The majority of cuts on the album run a lot longer than normal with Angus virtually taking over the show and turning every song into a boogie workout – triffic stuff!

The LP kicks off in grand style; good ol'Bon doing a nice line in Paul Hogan banter; ''Can I have your attention please. We're now on air and we'd like your participation; here's a song for ya called 'Live Wire', and from here on in the lads can do no wrong. Next up is 'Problem Child' (''this one's all about Angus''), followed by the excellent, 'high voltage', and if the tennis racquet is still in the cupboard by this point you need psychiatric care.

Then Bon comes out with a line that would do Woody Allen proud: ''You all come from New York City, is that not true, then this one's for you; 'Hell Ain't A

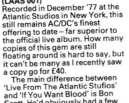

Bad Place To Be','' (couldn't agree more Bon). Side one runs for 25 mins 35 secs, longer than average, and the flip is almost as long clocking in at 20 mins 11 secs. When you consider that there's only three cuts on side two, 'The Jack', 'Whole Lotta Rosie' and 'The Rocker', thats just gotta be value for money.

DAVID WERNER
'David Werner Live'
(Epic AS690)
Whatever happened to David Werner? Same old story, I'm afraid. Right artiste, right time, wrong place; pity cos our David is a true artiste who deserves better than being consigned to cut-out bins round the country. I recall a colleague raving about DW so much so that I dashed outr to buy the studio LP and was immediately impressed, a delightful selection of AOR mayhem, reeking of good, ol' David Bowie gone HM.

Side one of 'DWL' was recorded in 'The Whiskey' LA on October 3 1979. Three cuts were culled from the original album, released incidentally in the same year '79, these being 'What Do You Need To Love', 'Can't Imagine' and 'Every New Romance', though there are two other numbers, 'Death Of Me Yet' and 'Aggravation Non Stop' that do not appear on the studio album.

Side two, meanwhile, is a total piss-take, a tribute to WBCN 104FM, which is a Boston-based radio station. If you've never heard any yankee radio then this album's worth buying just for this side. Everything you did, or did not want to hear, is condensed into a totally over-the-top eight minutes worth of garbage, ending with a studio cut 'Too Late To Cry', from the 'DW' album. A worthy addition to the 'Konnoisseurs' collection.

MOLLY HATCHET
'Molly Hatchet Live'
(Epic AS528)
Originally released as a deluxe, special collectors' boxed set, containing two copies of a five-track live album and a copy of the first Hatchet studio LP, this has gotta be one of my prized gems, and my collection boasts some pretty obscure stuff.

I still think Hatchet are the finest Southern band currently doing the rounds. I caught them at a 'Day On The Green' a couple of years ago and, on the evidence of that performance, I can safely say that no Confederate band comes close to these chicken-gitar-scratchin-wild-eyed-Southern-boys live, and that includes both Blackfoot and the Godfathers Lynyrd Skynyrd. There was a recent rumour that the MH's had split up, but I'm pleased to report that they're still very much alive. Not only have they managed to get

old singer Danny Joe[to replace the overwe[Farrar, but they've als[Bruce Crump the elbo[brought in Mother[skinsman, B.B. Q[en[prove an interesti[ng combination, both o[based in Atlanta, after[

The five live tracks[recorded at the Cap[Passaic, New Jersey[Reale and hearing th['Bounty Hunter' an[Country' performed i[it's surprising to find[still haven't released[Hatchet album. The oth[live toons are 'Big Apple['Dreams I'll Never See' [An Old Friend', and you[me, this is a classic wel[chasing.

STARZ
'Starz Live At The Mur[
Auditorium, Louisville[
1978, Superstars Rad[
Presents.
(Capitol, 8857/8858)
What is there left to say[Starz that hasn't been [already. Two of their [albums have already[this very colum, and[the Hellcats destined[megastars next year [this I hear about the B[Harkin / Joe X. Dube b[systems go on the St[as Commande[haw[say: 'anything o[next half hour'. In th[live offering, howeve[46 mins or so – of pu[

Much as I loved th[studio albums, the kil[was always lacking [part they suffered fr[production, which is ['SLATMA' is a must, [Starz favourites so[better live, with 'S[Times' and 'Sub[simply wizzing [fine axe work of [and Harkin. But th[this bunch is fro[Lee Smith – a gr[even better raps: [Louisville. All you g[listen. The other nig[first got to town this [Kentucky women ar[Kentucky race horse[real, real fast. But I te[last night back a th[had ourselves a [derby!'' Almost M[material ...

The best momen[album, however, c[through 'Waiting [our Michael shouts[gonna hear every f[riff ever recorded'[count three – 'Yo[Me', 'Satisfactio[a[Woman' – which le['Coliseum Rock', bo[the heaviest riffs eve[to vinyl. Perhaps th[unofficial live albu[m

18

and 'If You Want Blood...' is Bon Scott. He'd obviously had a few beers before recording 'LFTAS' and with the audience being distinctly on the small side, around 50 or so crammed into the studio, this is very much a trip down memory lane (remember when AC/DC used to play the Red Cow?). The majority of cuts on the album run a lot longer than normal, with Angus virtually taking over the show and turning every song into a boogie workout – triffic stuff!

'The LP kicks off in grand style; good ol' Bon doing a nice line in Paul Hogan banter: "Can I have your attention, please? We're now on air and we'd like your participation. Here's a song for ya called 'Live Wire'." And from here on in, the lads can do no wrong. Next up is 'Problem Child' ("This one's all about Angus"), followed by the excellent 'High Voltage', and if the tennis racquet is still in the cupboard by this point you need psychiatric care.

'Then Bon comes out with a line that would do Woody Allen proud: "You all come from New York City, is that not true? Then this one's for you – 'Hell Ain't A Bad Place To Be'." (Couldn't agree more, Bon.) Side One runs for 25 mins 35 secs, longer than average, and the flip is almost as long, clocking in at 20 mins 11 secs. When you consider that there's only three cuts on Side Two, 'The Jack', 'Whole Lotta Rosie' and 'The Rocker', that's just gotta be value for money.'

"There are two types of shows," mused Angus in *Sounds* as this first assault on the States wound down to its conclusion. "You can either be like performing seals and just have people sitting there gawking at you. Or you can have an all-in-together thing with the kids and us all having a good time."

The latter was certainly the AC/DC way. Moreover, Bon was taking a somewhat philosophical line as far as the boredom of the road was concerned.

"It can get to be a drag being in a different hotel room every night and not knowing where you put your toothbrush or a clean pair of drawers," he revealed to Sylvie Simmons during an interview for *Sounds*. "But what's the alternative? It's even more boring being stuck

'LIVE FROM THE ATLANTIC STUDIOS' IS REVIEWED IN *KERRANG!* IN 1983

AC/DC

LIVE
from the Atlantic

ATLANTIC

A

STE

PROMOTIONAL USE ONLY
NOT FOR SALE

in front of a conveyor belt at some factory every day of your life for the next 60 years, like a lot of the kids who come to see us – which is where we'd all be now if it wasn't for this life. So, I'd be stupid to knock it – it's great. And how can you get bored with so many different beautiful women around?!"

So, having made the first inroads in the American dream – and come out of it rather well – AC/DC hot-footed it back to Australia as the year ended, in order to start work on their next studio album. Once more, the production team of Vanda and Young had been retained. And again, Albert Studios was the chosen venue. The next album was to be an important one in the continuing upward rise of the band. Indeed, the coming year (1978) was one where the band had to make a leap to another level, if they were to be taken seriously as a long-term proposition...

THE SLEEVE FOR THE LEGENDARY 'LIVE FROM THE ATLANTIC STUDIOS' LP

CHAPTER SIX

A COMING OF AGE

"Angus Young is one of the reasons I started playing guitar in the first place. When I was young, I would dream of being Angus up onstage. I even wanted a Gibson guitar because he had one – not that I ever got it! AC/DC in general were certainly an early musical influence on me..."
– Dino Cazares (Fear Factory)

I t was 1978. The Punk Rock explosion was beginning to become something of a wheezing dinosaur in itself. All the early raw energy and anarchic music was starting to stagnate under the weight of expectations. The Sex Pistols had put a bullet through their own head. The Clash had shown themselves to be just another good Rock band. The Damned were a deliberate music hall joke of sorts. The Stranglers had become serious about their music. What price infamy and revolution now?

But AC/DC were in a very fortunate position. As the media began to take notice once more of the burgeoning Metal scene in the UK, Acca Dacca had already made inroads. Their following was diverse enough to straddle the Punk phenomenon and the perennial Metal scene. What's more, as one of the most vibrant hunting packs around, they were in a prime position to pick up young fans starting to get into HM.

These kids just didn't want hand-me-down heroes from elder brothers or dads. They wanted their own idols. Welcome to the birth of the AC/DC legend!

During February and March 1978, the band were locked in the studio with the perennial team of Vanda and Young (almost as synonymous with the band as Marks is with Spencer or Tom with Jerry at this juncture) busily preparing for what was going to be the most important album of their career.

Titled 'Powerage', the album was released in the UK on April 28, charting a month later. It reached the Top 30, but sadly peaked at Number 26, something of a let-down after the Top 20 success of 'Let There Be Rock'.

By and large critics took to the album, even though there was a feeling of *déja vu* here. Mark Putterford, assessing 'Powerage' in *Kerrang!* some six years later, had this to say:

'(The record) inevitably found the going tough when trying to match its famous predecessor. Really, it was just more of the same insistent drumming, rumbling bass, snarling vocals and chugging riffs. AC/DC had obviously decided that to change direction or even to broaden their musical scope now would be to disappoint their growing legions of fans, who saw them as the ultimate escapist band, and wanted nothing from them but that remorseless aural pummelling.'

UFO: THESE GUYS WERE ONCE MISTAKEN FOR AC/DC!

So, was this reasonable? Had Acca Dacca become nothing more than a parody of themselves? Frankly, it's unfair to criticise 'Powerage' too much. How can any album with songs like 'Sin City', 'Riff Raff' and 'What's Next To The Moon' be anything other than essential? The trouble was that AC/DC were in a no-win situation: stick to the tried and tested musical approach and you'd be accused of treading water. Change direction and you'd be accused of losing sight of your roots.

Sounds, though, was suitably ecstatic, describing the album as: 'Testimony to the rawest and most uncompromising sclerosis, no room for rebuttal'. Indeed, there was a sneaky logic in this record. It had sufficient Punk energy to appeal to fans of that genre, enough power and muscle to pick up fans of Metal, and abundant commerciality for the record company to see a hope of progression in the sales stakes. And let's not forget that 'Gimme A Bullet' verged on the Disco generation, such was the rhythmic tempo!

"Our writin' comes from life on the road really," Bon told *Sounds*' Sylvie Simmons. "Whatever comes into my brain when we're on the road I jot down (on a tape recorder), in order not to lose it. Usually I'm in a drunken state; when I listen to it back the next morning I think, 'Hey, did I say that?! Did I THINK that?'! But out of it you can usually get some pretty good road stuff."

"Our albums and music will never get orchestrated or ballady or that kind of mush," Angus protested to *Sounds*. "Our musical ambition is to put down a whole album like it was done by Little Richard back in the '50s, no double-tracking or anything. We may be little, but we make a lot of noise!"

Plans for AC/DC to set the promotional wheels back into motion with an extensive UK tour to coincide with the release of 'Powerage' were slightly affected when Angus picked up a niggling foot injury. The first three dates of this planned 28-date trek thus had to be pulled. But the rest fitted neatly into place, with the band receiving rapturous ovations across the country.

The support act for this tour were British Lions, regarded at the time as one of the fastest-rising bands in the UK. Formed from the ashes of Mott The Hoople, the quintet featured old Hoople stalwarts Overend Watts (bass), Morgan Fisher (keyboards) and Dale Griffin (drums), plus ex-Medicine Head vocalist John Fiddler and guitarist Ray Major. They signed a supposedly huge deal with Phonogram and issued their eponymous debut album in February 1978, two months prior to going out with AC/DC. But they never made any lasting impact, receiving a very lukewarm response on this tour.

The British dates finished up at the end of May in Scotland (Dundee, to be precise), after which AC/DC headed back to the States, where they were still struggling to make any commercial impact.

The band's US schedule called for tours at different times with Rainbow, British bluesters Savoy Brown, Alice Cooper, Journey and the Scorpions. Vocalist Klaus Meine of the last-named recalls that alliance with much fondness.

"It was our first proper tour of America. And going out on the road with AC/DC was a very pleasurable experience. The two bands became instant friends – a friendship that's lasted right up to this day.

"After the first date we did with them – I think it was in Texas – I went out for breakfast the following morning to a local eaterie. Anyway, as I sat there by myself who should wander in but Bon Scott? At that point we'd not been introduced, but he came up to me and said, 'Hi, I'm Bon. You're in the Scorpions, aren't you?'. We had a good chat that morning and got on very well. But that was typical of the man. He was always so friendly to everyone."

The band's live reputation throughout the States was growing with almost every gig. They might not yet have managed to make any chart breakthrough, but the Aussies' popularity as a road-hardened battalion could not be denied.

Of course, it wasn't always sweetness and light for them out there. In Detroit, Malcolm Young got into a nasty altercation with a local promoter when the latter tried to pull the plug on Acca Dacca because they'd supposedly exceeded the 98 decibel noise limit. This led to some damage to the band's equipment and a near-arrest for them. Malcolm, bringing to mind the Kiss klassik 'Detroit Rock City', disparagingly remarked to *Sounds*: "Detroit a rock 'n' roll city? There's more happening in Tasmania!"

Perhaps the most famous story to come out of this particular US tour concerned Bon. It was alleged that he went to the toilet and found himself standing next to an employee of Atlantic Records. The latter asked Bon whether he was AC or DC, to which Bon, according to legend, replied: "Neither, I'm the lightning flash in the middle!" Bon then punched out the somewhat startled chap.

Over the following couple of years, Bon was asked about that incident on more than one occasion. He always gave a knowing, enigmatic smirk but would never actually confirm or deny this publicly, all of which just added to the myth of the incident.

In Philadelphia, British band UFO were mistaken for

RUDY SCHENKER: A CLOSE MATE OF AC/DC

AC/DC! What happened was that the two bands were appearing together at The Tower Theater and a number of luminaries from Atlantic's New York office had made the two-hour drive up to Philly from the Big Apple. UFO went on first, and after their set vocalist Phil Mogg and bassist Pete Way went into the AC/DC dressing room to socialise. Then it happened.

An Atlantic executive approached Phil Mogg and, in front of Acca

Dacca, said: "Bon, what a great show!" That's on a par with the EMI employee who once asked Pink Floyd, "By the way, which one's Pink?"

Touring with UFO provided AC/DC not only with a co-headlining situation with one of the hottest Hard Rock bands around at the time, but also cemented a lasting friendship between two bands who

shared very similar musical outlooks. Angus and Malcolm even gave UFO's rhythm guitarist/keyboardsman Paul Raymond the nickname of Shirley Bassey because of the ludicrously bright clothes he'd wear.

Years later, Pete Way recalled: "Touring with AC/DC was great for both bands. We drew a hardcore audience who weren't into hit singles bands, but wanted the sort of Hard Rock music that both

AC/DC '78 (FROM LEFT): MALCOLM, BON, CLIFF, ANGUS, PHIL

bands delivered."

For AC/DC this period of their life was a dogged cycle: travel-hotel-gig-travel-hotel-gig, etc. But they seemed to relish this lifestyle, it being the only way they could possibly break through in the biggest record buying market in the world.

"When the kids come to see us, they want to rock – that's it. To be part of this big mass thing with the band," affirmed Angus to *Sounds*. "You watch. I'll hit a chord on the guitar and right down there at the front there'll be a hundred kids hitting it right along with you, going through the motions like they were up there onstage with you, which I guess is where they would be if they could. They're really no different to us.

"Back in Australia we were like your average kid into rock 'n' roll from a small town sort of background. We were like the outcasts or whatever, always getting into trouble with the cops and picked on because we had long hair and didn't dress like them. But we made it onto the stage and they (the fans) are still trying to get there, or at least dreaming and fantasising about it.

"We haven't forgotten what it was like and we are definitely on the kids' side."

In all, the band played nearly 100 shows during this period in the States, ranging from small clubs to an appearance at the prestigious Day On The Green outdoor festival in San Francisco during August. But it was beginning to work. Thanks to all of this hard graft, with little or no support from the media out in the States, sales of the 'Powerage' album had actually risen to close on the quarter-of-a-million mark – an amazing success story for a band who had done it all their own way by touring, touring, touring until they were ready to drop. And Atlantic now woke up, realising they were sitting on a potential goldmine!

Back in the UK, AC/DC's stock was sent rising by their first success in the singles chart. 'Rock 'N' Roll Damnation' was issued in seven-inch and the newly popular 12-inch vinyl formats during May 1978. Strangely, this was a track not even to be found on the 'Powerage' album, but then maybe this was the shrewd thinking

FROM PAGE 24

of the songs that didn't quite make it into the band's live repertoire, like 'Overdose' and 'Dog Eat Dog'.

There's no need to keep this in cling-film, it'll stay fresh forever!

'POWERAGE' ATLANTIC K50483 APRIL '78

A YEAR, a European and American tour, several million new fans and a new bass player (Cliff Williams) later, the crazy Kangaroos were back in Albert Studios, Sydney with Vanda and Young to record their new LP.

'Powerage' inevitably found the going tough when trying to match its famous predecessor. Really, it was just more of the same insistent drumming, rumbling bass, snarling vocals and chugging riffs. AC/DC had obviously decided that to change direction or even to broaden their musical scope now would be to disappoint their growing legions of fans who saw them as the ultimate escapist band and wanted nothing more from them but that remorseless aural pummelling.

I didn't really get into 'Powerage'; I didn't have 'Let There Be Rock' off the turntable long enough! But it's good, solid, engaging AC/DC doing what they know best and the pace barely slackens from 'Gimme A Bullet', 'Down Payment Blues' and 'Sin City' right through to 'Up To My Neck In You', 'What's Next To The Moon' and 'Kicked In The Teeth'.

Fave track has to be the glorious rabid rock 'n' roll of 'Riff Raff', which had the demented satchel-wielding schoolboy going berserk and proving that he could still whip up quite a fretboard frenzy even within the padded wall confines of a recording studio.

'IF YOU WANT BLOOD . . . YOU'VE GOT IT' ATLANTIC K50532 OCTOBER '78

BUT PLAYING live was, and always will be, AC/DC's forté and around this time I shared with many the boundless energy and intense excitement of AC/DC gigs. As if I needed it (of course I did!), the band recorded a number of summer shows during their 1978 World Tour and channelled them into this single live album – their only official suchlike release so far.

The cover showed a bloody Angus impaled on his guitar, and while the spectacular AC/DC live show hadn't quite gone to such extremes yet, the album did the impossible and translated the band's electrifying show onto vinyl.

They're all here: 'Riff Raff', 'Hell Ain't A Bad Place To Be', 'Bad Boy Boogie', 'The Jack', 'Problem Child', 'Whole Lotta Rosie', the last single 'Rock 'N' Roll Damnation', 'High Voltage', 'Let There Be Rock' and 'Rocker'.

Thankfully, the album was kept singular (a double album of AC/DC would be a bit too much to digest, let's face it!) and for me it represented the band at a peak. A descent looked menacing . . .

'HIGHWAY TO HELL' ATLANTIC K50628 JULY '79

COINCIDENTLY, THE band themselves seemed to feel it was time for a change as well and decided to split with their old production team of Vanda and Young to rope in Robert John 'Mutt' Lange to twiddle the knobs. They also chose to record in London's Roundhouse Studios this time around and emerged in the summer clutching 'Highway To Hell'.

Probably produced with one eye squinting across the Atlantic at our Coca-Cola cousins, the album was more polished and streamlined, including more backing vocals and a more precise delivery.

But basically, it was just the same old AC/DC stompin' steadily through 'Highway To Hell', 'Shot Down In Flames', 'Get It Hot' and 'Love Hungry Man'. Raising the tempo for 'Girl's Got Rhythm', 'Walk All Over You', 'Beating Around The Bush' and 'If You Want Blood'. And lowering it for 'Night Prowler'.

Sadly, Angus' innocent pose

AC/DC's CURRENT (geddit?) line-up (from left): Cliff Williams, Malcolm Young, Simon Wright, Angus Young, Brian Johnson.

as the devil on the front cover and the inclusion of the tragically prophetic 'Touch Too Much' were to prove cruel ironies. This was to be Bon's last vinyl outing as he died seven months later. His heavy drinking had sent him on his own highway to hell, and a touch too much one night resulted in him choking on his own vomit.

I stashed the album away and left AC/DC for dead.

'BACK IN BLACK' ATLANTIC K50735 JULY '80

IGNORANTLY, I by-passed 'BIB' and the next album, 'For Those About To Rock', for reasons that remain unclear.

It wasn't until recently that I brought myself to face with 'BIB' and subsequently 'FTATR' and discovered that absence really DOES make the heart grow fonder.

Brian 'Beano' Johnson, the ex-Geordie geordie (if ya see what I mean!) was the chap chosen to replace Bon, and his parrotesque vocals didn't seem a bit out of place as the new AC/DC rocketed back in style.

The sombre black cover and the eerie chiming of a huge bell at the start of 'Hell's Bells' seemed to mourn for Bon, but the band didn't dwell on nostalgia and presented a new-look AC/DC that coupled that ol' raunchy stomp with a touch of commercialism.

Recorded in Nassau with 'Mutt' Lange and under the management of Peter Mensch, AC/DC were BIG stars now. I've grown to love the album. Before, sometimes, you could plonk the needle down anywhere and it would sound much the same, but here every song has more individuality. From 'What Do You Do For Money Honey' and 'Let Me Put My Love Into You' to 'You Shook Me All Night Long' and 'Rock 'N' Roll Ain't Noise Pollution', it's all classy, uplifting stuff.

'FOR THOSE ABOUT TO ROCK . . . WE SALUTE YOU' ATLANTIC K580851 NOVEMBER '81

THE ONCE sleazy, dirty AC/DC were now a classy, highly-tuned rock machine. But again the music didn't cruise on superstar

pretensions as the band recorded their new album in Paris, once more with 'Mutt' Lange at the helm.

Where once was a one-and-a-half ton bell, there was now an arsenal (spit again) of cannons which saluted those of us about to rock. And plenty of us did to the slick 'n' shiny newies from Young, Young and Johnson like 'Put The Finger On You', 'Let's Get It Up', 'Evil Walks' and 'COD'.

However, 'For Those . . .' didn't quite match 'BIB' and several of the songs didn't work for me, as the band appeared to be searching for new ideas. 'Breaking The Rules' and 'Night Of The Long Knives' were below par, while 'Spellbound' was just rather tedious.

But then . . .

'FLICK OF THE SWITCH' ATLANTIC 780 100-1 AUGUST '83

. . . OBLITERATING ANY doubters came the highly-charged 'Flick Of The Switch', straight from Compass Point Studios in Nassau to the brain in your skull.

Apparently, the lads decided to drop Lange's lighter, cleaner sound and roll back the years to the raw, abrasive crunch of the old AC/DC. So they had a bash at producing themselves and fathered this crushing, EXTREMELY high-voltaged output.

In places, the rough 'n' ready production gives the elpee a almost demo-feel and that must be music to the ears of those who feared AC/DC were letting up. Cop a lugload of 'Landslide', 'This House Is On Fire', 'Flick Of The Switch' or 'Brain Shake', and you'll sleep peacefully.

My personal favourites would probably be 'Bedlam In Belgium', 'Nervous Shakedown' and 'Guns For Hire', which prove that, even after so many years, AC/DC are still as irresistible as always.

Listen to the start of 'Guns For Hire' and you'll hear that pale, boney hand jerk across the live wires. You'll visualise that screwed-up brat face and the ever-present schoolboy uniform that accompanies it. You'll be able to feel the rising power as the legs twitch and the head nods faster and faster . . .

AC/DC'S '78 UK TOUR PROGRAMME

behind Atlantic's plans: to ensure that every AC/DC fan would buy the single for this unavailable cut and thereby ensure a healthy chart position. Whatever, it worked. The single reached Number 24, with 'Sin City' on the B-side.

In fact, there was to be the rather ludicrous sight of Acca Dacca performing the song on 'Top Of The Pops'! Those privileged to see the band headbanging furiously in front of the rather bemused studio audience still treasure the memory.

And the band also pulled a fast one on the BBC. In those days, every act booked to appear on the programme had to re-record the song in question, and then mime to a playback. But AC/DC weren't impressed with such shenanigans. They felt the original studio recording should suffice. So, to this end they 'agreed' to the BBC's demands, went into Basing Street Studios in London – and did nothing!

The band simply went through the motions of re-recording the song, when in fact nothing had been taped. They then gave 'Top Of The Pops' a tape of the original version, which was subsequently aired. AC/DC dutifully mimed to it, although Bon did his best to send the whole ludicrous affair up by lip-synching very badly (deliberately, it's been suggested). Mind you, there were precious few clips of the singer screened. Most of the shots were of Angus cavorting around in his shorts.

What all of this meant was that by the time the band stepped back out on the road in Europe during the last couple of months of 1978, they were hot and happening news. AC/DC were on the verge of the big breakthrough. And Atlantic wasted no time in underpinning this hard-won success. Next on the agenda was a live album – one they felt sure would take AC/DC to the next level. They weren't wrong...

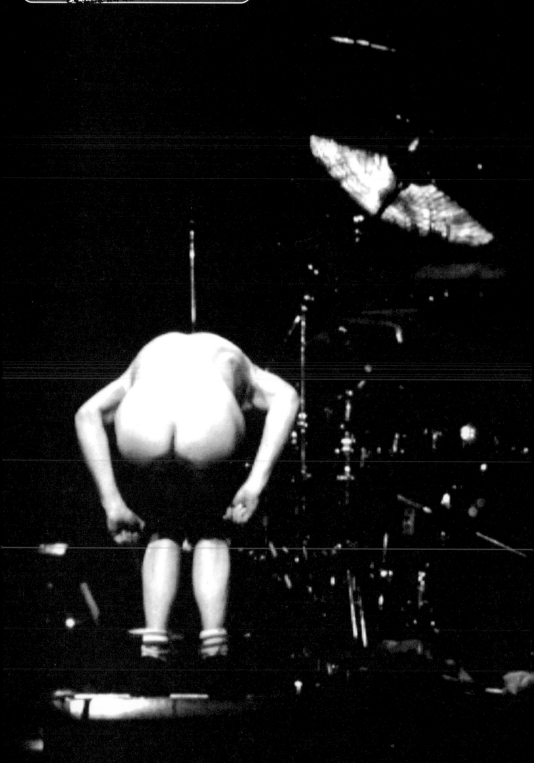

CHAPTER SEVEN

ALL HELL BREAKIN' LOOSE

"I first heard AC/DC in 1978 or 1979. It was the song 'Let There Be Rock'. And I have to admit that at first I didn't like Bon's vocals. But then I went out and bought the album of the same title. Within a couple of weeks Bon was my favourite vocalist, because he was just so different! And Angus and Malcolm just rule. In fact, Malcolm is one of my biggest influences as a rhythm guitarist. I also liked the fact that they were short!"
– Scott Ian (Anthrax)

In October 1978, Atlantic Records decided to go for the most obvious AC/DC album of them all – a live effort. Titled 'If You Want Blood... You've Got It' (a tribute to the band's no-holds-barred approach to stage work), this was a quite magnificent effort that crystallised the band's true worth and talents. At the time, one couldn't have wished for any more appropriate album from a group who'd made their name onstage.

Mark Putterford had this to say about the album in *Kerrang!*: 'Playing live was, and always will be, AC/DC's *forté* and around this time I shared with many the boundless energy and intense excitement of AC/DC gigs. The band recorded a number of Summer shows during their 1978 World Tour and channelled them into this single live album...

'The cover showed a bloody Angus impaled on his guitar, and whilst the spectacular AC/DC live show hadn't quite gone to such extremes yet, the album did the impossible and translated the band's electrifying show onto vinyl.

'They're all here: 'Riff Raff', 'Hell Ain't A Bad Place To Be', 'Bad Boy Boogie', 'The Jack', 'Problem Child', 'Whole Lotta Rosie', 'Rock 'N' Roll Damnation', 'High Voltage', 'Let There Be Rock' and 'The Rocker'.

'Thankfully, the album was kept singular (a double album of AC/DC would be a bit too much to digest)... and for me it represented the band at a peak.'

Inevitably, 'If You Want Blood...' proved to be the band's biggest UK album to date, peaking at Number 13 – and if America wasn't exactly following suit, then the record did well enough Stateside to convince the powers-that-be that here was a band still striking out for fresh commercial pastures, and succeeding in their endeavours.

A maxi-single, available in both seven-inch and 12-inch formats, was issued by Atlantic shortly after the album, combining live renditions of 'Whole Lotta Rosie' and 'Hell Ain't A Bad Place To Be'. This helped augment the band's legend, by establishing the former track as one of the most potent and popular in the history of Heavy Metal music.

AC/DC promoted the live album by heading straight out on tour in the UK during early November for a series of 16 dates in just 18

SOUNDS ANNOUNCES THAT INFAMOUS WHO GIG, 1979

WHO NAME THE DAY

THE WHO will be playing an open-air gig at Wembley Stadium on August 18 after all. The on-off gig, which has been the subject f much speculation and denial in recent eeks, was confirmed by a spokesperson for e Who shortly before *Sounds* went to ess.

It will be the Who's major British appearance this year although they could well play more isolated one-offs as they already have in London, Glasgow and Edinburgh.

Ticket details have not yet been finalised but they should be announced next week. An all-star line-up is also being got together for the all-day festival and although there are no confirmed acts as yet the Boomtown Rats were leading the rumour stakes on Monday evening.

STRANGLERS: can Wembley expect sights like this?

Stranglers, AC/DC, Lofgren in Who bash

Minds over matter

SIMPLE MINDS have a British tour following th of their 'Chelsea Girl' sin Zoom.

THE STRANGLERS, AC/DC and NILS LOFGREN will be supporting the Who at their Wembley Stadium open air gig on August 18.

This will be the Stranglers first English gig this year although they headed the bill at the Scottish Loc Festiv in

their next studio album which is now complete and will be released by United Artists early in September.

AC/DC will also have a new album our shortly on Atlantic and Nils Lofgren recently rel an album o will be h

at £8.00 in advance. A full list of outlets was published in last week's Sounds.

Pete Townshend, who last week announced a solo deal with Atco, has now finalised the line-up of his band to appear at this Friday's Rock Against Racism at the Rainbo in alb

They open at Chesterfie sion Club on July 12 and the Jacksdale Grey Topper 13, Ajanta Club 19, Blackpoo breck Castle 20, Dudley J Newport Stowaway 25, S Limit Club 26, Liverpool E Leeds Ffor e Grene Ho London M Machine 30 burgh Ge Square

AC/DC ARE CONFIRMED ON THE WHO BILL, SOUNDS, '79

days! Extra nights were slotted in everywhere along the way, as the band literally exploded in popularity. They were now a major act, one to be taken very seriously indeed. They were already using stage effects, such as smoke canisters hidden inside Angus' perennially present satchel and a walkway running behind Rudd's drum kit, which provided Angus and Bon with the opportunity to stretch their legs!

Of course, not everything ran smoothly. Right at the start of the tour, Bon got lost at the Glasgow Apollo whilst trying to find his way to the stage. By some quirk of fate he ended up outside the venue, and had a very hard time explaining to the naturally unconvinced bouncers that he was the singer in the headlining band! Eventually, Bon's gift of the gab persuaded the Scots security team that the story was so

87

AC/DC
'Highway To Hell'
(Atlantic K50628)****

CHUNG-CHUNGA-Chung-
Chunga and the riff is
introduced. Whaaaarrrgh! And
here comes Bon Scott on vocals
and muscle flexing (this bloke is
so butch he shaves the soles of
his feet'). Yeah-Yeah-Yeah-
Waaaarrrgh and it's a quick
chorus from the rest of the
band and then . . . and then it's
Kertraaaang' The Angus Spot.
This maelstrom of guitar
thrashing from schoolboy
fetishist Andy Young is so
much a permanent feature of
any AC/DC track that, in the
interests of brevity, it will
hitherto be referred to as 'The AS'.
   And that, music lovers, is the
fundamental basis of all
AC/DC's oeuvre. The chords
may be changed occasionally to
protect the ignorant, there may
be an extra chorus here and
there and 'The AS' may vary in
both length and intensity, but
that, essentially, is their musical
masterplan in a nutcase, oops,
nutshell. Don't get me wrong. I
come to praise AC/DC not
bury them; after all, doing the
heavy metal boogie album after
album and still managing to
make it sound like a good time
is no mean feat.
   As you should have deduced
by now, 'Highway To Hell'
marks no adventurous new
ground-breaking by AC/DC;
they haven't gone disco (eat
your hearts out Kiss fans,
snicker), they haven't footled
around with reggae or jazz,
there isn't even a syndrum to be
heard. No, this is the AC/DC
you already know and love hate
— all thud-crunch kerraang-
whaarrgh. Music to knock
walls by.
   My only grumble with
AC/DC has always been over
Bon Scott's lassitudes in the
larynx department. He has
often sounded like Alex Harvey
on a bad night to me; always
opting for the chest beating,
primeval scream at the expense
of harmony, screeching to keep
his head above the choppy seas

of Angus's Force 10 guitar gale.
It's a shame really, 'cos
there's definitely more to him
than just a loud bellow, a
malevolent leer and a couple of
tattoos, as he proves during the
course of 'Love Hungry Man',
this album's closest to a
sensitive track and sounding
rather like Free meets Led Zep
and even featuring some vocal
double-tracking (a rare studio
frippery for a band who prefer
to keep their live and recorded
identities as close as possible),
while maintaining the thud-

thud-'AS'-whaarrgh standard.
   Lyrically too, this album is
very much in the well-thumbed
AC/DC guide to mysogyny, a
large proportion of their songs
revolving around the outsize
attributes of some old tart
they've abused and probably
been infected by somewhere
back down the road. I mean,
titles like 'Walk All Over You',
'Beating Around The Bush',
'Get It Hot' and 'Night
Prowler' are hardly likely to
herald sensitive tales of true and
everlasting love between man

Chunga-Ch
Kerrraa

bands as stylised as AC/D
Do they risk alienating th
existing fans and try som
new just for the sake of a
grab at musical credibility,
do they carry on churning it c
hoping to ride out the almost
inevitable critical backlash?
Very few have had the skill or
originality to achieve the form
(Beatles, Stones) and just as f
have had the perseverance a
consistency to carry off th
latter (Quo, Sabbath, Floyd),
AC/DC are one of the few.
DAVID LEW

...han are they?
...isn't Scott's vo
...des, nor the Allbran
...ty of that three-headed
...machine of Rudd,
...and Williams around
...he AC/DC ferris wheel
...s but, of course, 'The
...nd rather like a
...und roundabout, the
...watcher might think it a
...l watching/hearing the
...old faces/riffs going
...and round in a blur of
...remembrance.
...a quandry faced by all

ga-Waaaarrrgh-
gg! (part 94)

Pic by David Hill

SOUNDS' REVIEW
OF 'HIGHWAY TO
HELL', 1979

improbable, he must be telling the truth. A laughing Bon told *Sounds* a couple of days later: "I can't remember that. It was two days ago!"

But this was all to prove the end of an era for AC/DC. Their staunchest and longest serving allies, Harry Vanda and George Young, were about to part company with the band, as they moved on to fresh pastures and lifted their eyes towards new horizons.

At the suggestion of Atlantic in the States, Acca Dacca reluctantly shook hands with V&Y and headed out to Florida to work with legendary English producer Eddie Kramer. But things just didn't work out. Kramer, who in the past had been associated with such greats as Jimi Hendrix, Kiss and Led Zeppelin, had a style and manner of working that simply didn't gel at all with the more down-to-earth

89

AC/DC lads. Indeed, at more than one point in the early pre-production proceedings, members of the band nearly came to blows with Kramer. No, if the band were gonna make the record everyone was expecting, and hoping for, then Kramer would have to be canned.

Thus, manager Michael Browning took the bold decision to change producers. Into the breach stepped the less famous but fast-rising Robert John 'Mutt' Lange. A Rhodesian by birth, 'Mutt' had moved to the UK with his then-wife Stevie to try and forge a touring/ recording career as a duo. Sadly, this failed (Stevie has since made a hugely successful career for herself as a session singer). Lange, though, found his feet in the studio, starting out as an engineer before graduating to become a fully-fledged producer, working with the likes of the Boomtown Rats, The Motors and Graham Parker, all connected in some way with the high-profile New Wave. But he'd never worked with a band of AC/DC's style before.

So, why did the band go for such an untried producer? Simple. He was Michael Browning's flatmate in New York! With time of the essence and the need to find a suitable producer becoming increasingly urgent, Browning offered the job to Lange almost as a last-ditch effort. What a moment of inspiration.

Angus put it rather more simply, when he spoke to *Sounds*' Phil Sutcliffe: "Someone suggested Robert John, er, Lang... Langer... Lanj, you know."

Lange took up the challenge, moving with the band into the Roundhouse Studios in Chalk Farm, London to start work on what was to be a watershed album for AC/DC. Thus here were the band facing the end of the '70s with a new producer, new studio and an increased recording budget. But the attitude remained unaltered. The album, finished early in '79, was full of classic songs that have since become the standards by which others have subsequently been judged.

"It was a good learning period for all of us," Angus told Sutcliffe. "But in particular he done a good job on Bon's vocals..."

The album, titled 'Highway To Hell' (taking its monicker from Angus' description of America), was mixed by engineer Tony Platt in Ladbroke Grove. When it was finished, there was a portentous sense of achievement in the air. Here indeed were AC/DC starting out gloriously on Phase II of their career. But they were about to make another significant change, when manager Browning was ditched in favour of the mighty CCC organisation, based in New York.

Contemporary Communications Corps was a mighty and powerful beast at the time, looking after such major acts as Ted Nugent, Aerosmith and the Scorpions. In Hard Rock and Heavy Metal terms they were 'it' on the managerial front. They wielded a great deal of power – and didn't have failures. With Peter Mensch from CCC as their personal manager, Acca Dacca strode purposefully into the States during the Spring of 1979, ready to headline their way into the big time.

The band toured relentlessly around America, supported by the likes of guitar hero Pat Travers, Sammy Hagar and up-and-coming bands Riot and Blackfoot. However, it was AC/DC's stint with Southern Boogie masters Molly Hatchet in Texas that provided the most ridiculous stories for the media.

Sounds carried news of how Hatchet guitarist Dave Hlubek had come onstage in San Antonio during Acca Dacca's set – dressed up as a schoolboy. And, given Hlubek's extreme girth, the whole sight was apparently hilarious. And at the post-gig party, Bon got so wrecked that he actually drank a whole bottle in one go. Unfortunately, the bottle in question happened to be aftershave!

At this juncture, Bon would go on regular benders with members of Molly Hatchet or his own road crew, returning in a complete state at all hours. At this time it was all probably seen as harmless fun by the other members of the band. But given the fact that, barely a few months later, Bon was to die as a result of an extreme alcoholic binge, one can't help but wonder whether he was beginning to slip out of control. Had he passed the point of no return?

In fact, there was one moment on this leg of the tour when Bon caused panic by disappearing for a day, whilst the band were *en route* from California to Texas. The plane stopped over in Phoenix, Arizona for refuelling – and so did Bon. The band were forced to travel on to Austin for the planned show without the absent frontman. To make it worse, they had no idea whether he would actually turn up for the gig!

True to form, Bon did show up – he never actually missed a gig for

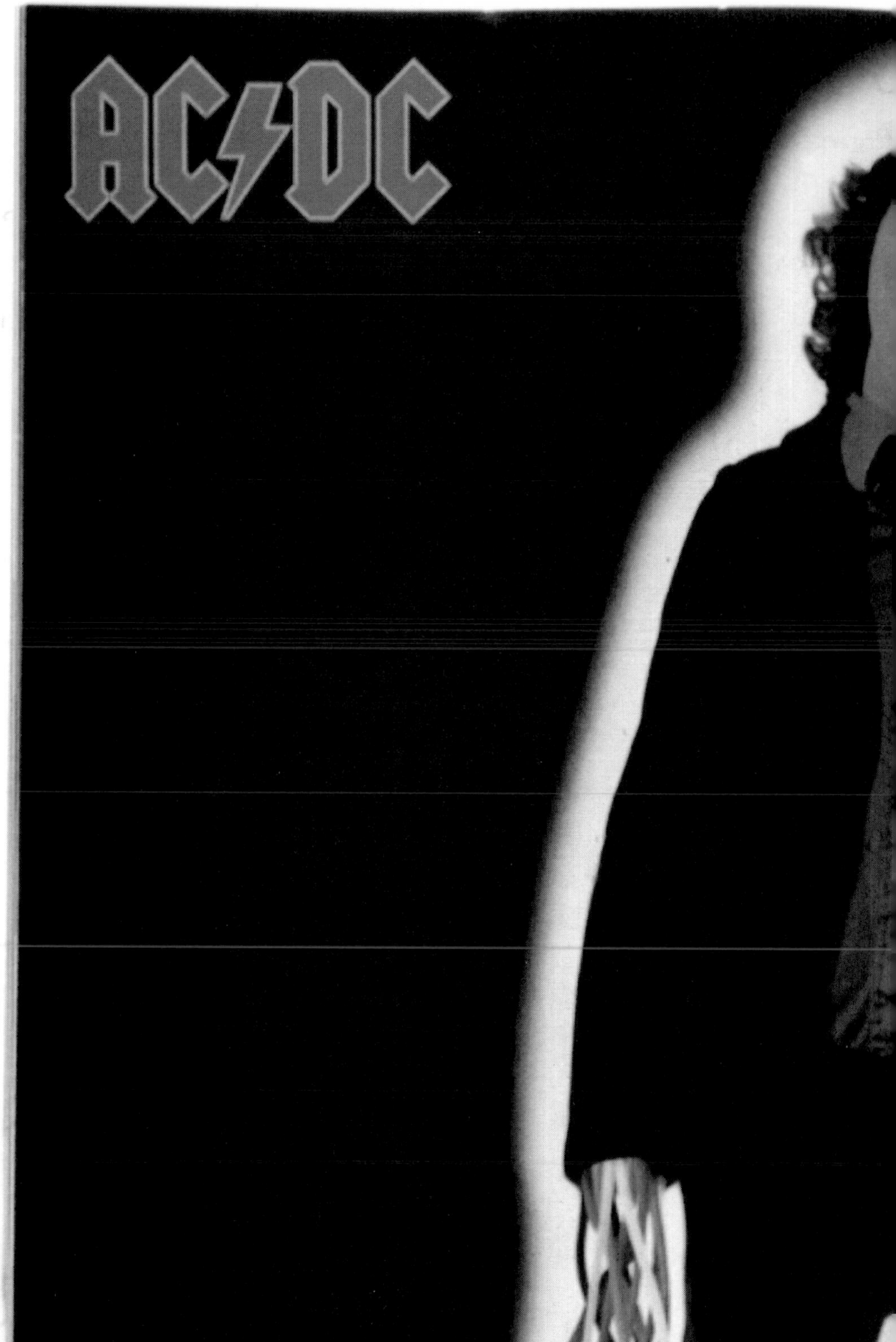
AC/DC

THE CLASSIC
'HIGHWAY TO HELL'
POSTER FROM
KERRANG!

KERRANG!

August 1979 SOUNDS

AC/DC

BOOMTOWN RATS

XTC

UK SUBS

Toura, Toura, Toura

Blondie, Rats, XTC, UK Subs, AC/DC, Oyster Cult all plan dates

AFTER A SLUGGISH rock and roll summer — enlivened by four major open-air festivals during August — there looks like being a crowded onslaught on the circuit during the autumn.

Leading the way later this month will be a mod package featuring **The Purple Hearts.** Dates are now being lined up and should be announced within a week or two.

In September the **UK Subs,** who've been among the most successful new bands this year in building up a following across country, will be touring to tie in with the release of the first album on Gem Records. And **XTC,** who'll be releasing their third album around then, will also be out on the road.

The Boomtown Rats will begin what looks like being an extensive British trek late in September and hopefully their third album will be released during the tour.

Budgie have returned from America — a venture that has proved less than successful as the band are now without a record deal having been dropped by A&M — and they'll be playing da in September, the rumour being that it is to be a farewell tour.

October sees tours by **Gillan** — who may finally have releas a new album by then — and **Robin Trower,** who is now based America and is working on his next album at the moment.

Continuing in the heavy metal vein, **AC/DC** will be undertak their first tour for more than a year. Their new album called 'Highway To Hell' was released last month. **The Ruts** are also lining up dates for October which will follow the release of the first album on Virgin.

Bill Nelson's Red Noise will be on the road in November w their second album in the shops and **John Miles** will be playin gigs around the same time.

This is in addition to visits from major acts durin the autum **Boston's** first ever British da s were anno ced week and B ie

RECORD   *Farewell Vivas*

LEED? CLUB, w

SOUNDS CONFIRMS AC/DC'S '79 TOUR

the band, whatever his state of health – recounting a strange tale of how he'd followed an attractive young lady off the flight, and... well, let's leave the explanation to Bon as recounted to Phil Sutcliffe of *Sounds*:

"We'd been drinking in the airport bar for about 10 minutes when I says, 'Don't you think it's time we caught our plane?' and she says, 'What do you mean our plane? I'm stayin' here'. I runs back and the f★★kin' flight's gone.

"Anyway, she takes me to this back bar – she was Mexican – and I starts drinkin' and playin' pool. I had a good night, beatin' every bastard. After about two hours I'm playin' this big-titted black chick and beatin' her too when I happen to look around and the whole bar is goin' 'Grrr'.

"I thinks, 'Uh-oh Bon', gives her another game and loses 9-1. 'Anyone else want to beat me?' I says. So I escapes with me life, only barely – and I made it to the gig in Austin."

The only other member of the band to actually display rather eccentric behaviour at this point in time was Phil Rudd. He indulged his increasing wealth by taking up hobbies such as Scalextric, flying in a huge set which he'd put up in the hotel room next to his own. When he got fed up with this hobby, he switched to photography. But he didn't just buy an Instamatic. Oh no. He'd book a second hotel room everywhere he went, which was turned into an elaborate dark room – at considerable expense!

The other three – Angus, Malcolm and Cliff – led very quiet, simple lives, leaving the debauchery and excess to Bon and Phil!

During this period, the band were even offered the chance to star in the horror movie 'Dracula Rocks'. But they weren't interested.

"We're not actors," Angus told Sylvie Simmons in *Sounds.* "We're too crazy. We'll let the Mick Jaggers go and make fools of themselves!"

Second choice after AC/DC? Queen!

"Freddie Mercury thought it was an insult to his teeth!" laughed Angus at the news. "Queen didn't like that. What? Gettin' AC/DC's cast-off roles?"

Eventually, the Boomtown Rats accepted the offer.

On July 27, 1979, 'Highway To Hell' was

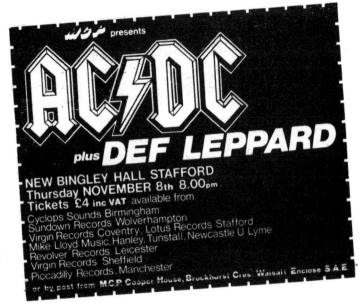

A *SOUNDS* AD FOR AC/DC'S '79 UK TOUR

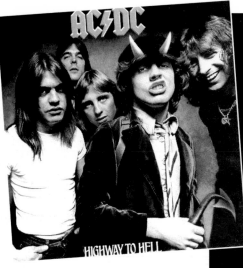

AC/DC '79 AND, LEFT, THE CLASSIC 'HIGHWAY TO HELL' SLEEVE

finally issued. It received considerable and worthy acclaim. With 'Mutt' Lange in tow, the band had succeeded in delivering a state-of-the-art album that was still utterly melodic and simplistic. All of the band's inestimable trademarks were intact, but they'd now been fleshed out with a formidable, inviting sound quality that left most of their rivals floundering. This was truly the first time that 'Mutt's studio genius had been allowed to flourish. Yet, it never swamped AC/DC's crucial spontaneity.

Dave Lewis raved about the album in *Sounds*:

'Chunga-chunga-chunga-chunga and the riff is introduced. Whaaaarrrgh! And here comes Bon Scott on vocals and muscle flexing (this bloke is so butch he shaves the soles of his feet!). Yeah-yeah-yeah-waaaarrrgh and it's a quick chorus from the rest of the band and then... and then it's Kerrrraaaang! The Angus Spot...

'And that, music lovers, is the fundamental basis of all AC/DC's *oeuvre*... 'Highway To Hell' marks no adventurous new ground-breaking by AC/DC; they haven't gone Disco; they haven't fooled around with Reggae or Jazz; there isn't even a syndrum to be heard. No, this is the AC/DC you already know and love/hate – all thrud-crunch-kerraang-and-whaarrrgh. Music to knock down walls by.'

To this day, 'Highway To Hell' remains arguably 'Mutt' Lange's finest work – and probably AC/DC's into the bargain.

The album strong-armed its way into the UK Top 10, peaking at Number Eight, whilst in the States it broke through into the Top 20, reaching Number 17. A triumph. At last, the band were an internationally successful proposition. They even enjoyed a minor US hit single thanks to the title track of the album, which reached a respectable Number 47 in August.

From the vantage point of more than a decade-and-a-half, 'Highway To Hell' still sends shivers down the spine like very little else from this era. In 1984, Mark Putterford re-assessed the album thus in *Kerrang!*:

'Probably produced with one eye squinting across the Atlantic at our Coca-Cola cousins, the album was more polished and stream-lined, including more backing vocals and a more precise delivery.

'But, basically, it was just the same old AC/DC stompin' steadily through 'Highway To Hell', 'Shot Down In Flames', 'Get It Hot' and 'Love Hungry Man'. Raising the tempo for 'Girls Got Rhythm', 'Walk All Over You', 'Beating Around The Bush' and 'If You Want Blood'. And lowering it for 'Night Prowler'.

'Sadly, Angus' innocent pose as the devil on the front cover and the inclusion of the tragically prophetic 'Touch Too Much' were to prove cruel ironies.'

In later years, 'Night Prowler' was to cause considerable discomfort for the band, when American serial killer Richard Ramirez claimed it as some form of perverted inspiration for his nocturnal

MORE SONGS ABOUT HUMPING AND BOOZE

HAVE AC/DC
GONE DISCO?
'NAH' SNARLS
PHILTHY
PHIL
SUTCLIFFE

99

activities. But at the time, who cared? AC/DC were throwing the ultimate late '70s party – and we were all invited.

On August 18, AC/DC returned to Britain to play the biggest show of their career thus far in the UK. It was at Wembley Stadium in London – known universally as the home of football. Headlining on the day were The Who, particular favourites with Angus. And, in typical Who style, the full bill was something of a musical pot pourri.

Opening up was American Nils Lofgren, a guitarist/vocalist most known for his work with Neil Young in the seminal Crazy Horse line-up and also renowned for using a trampoline as part of his stage set! Something decidedly different, but also reasonably well received. Next up were hot New Wave act The Stranglers, whose mix of dirty riffs, petrol-bomb melodies and darkly psychedelic keyboards had already established them as one of Britain's most popular outfits. They were certainly a valuable addition to proceedings, but still didn't really get the huge crowd revved up for action. It took AC/DC to do that.

Phil Sutcliffe summed 'em up thus in *Sounds*:

'They may never be exactly fashionable but AC/DC are in serious danger of becoming one of the world's great Rock bands. For illustration, I'll just describe the fourth song in their set, a wonderful rendering of 'Bad Boy Boogie'.

'As if he thought matters been a little tame to date, Angus opened the number by sprinting across the stage, flinging himself on the floor and flailing himself round in circles, all the while playing a berserk solo. Okay, we were listening. Then AC/DC played the most inspiring hard and heavy (song) you could imagine, so strong, so satisfying I'd even call it moving – the shivers and prickling of the scalp it gave me were the same symptoms of internal ecstasy I get from Joan Armatrading's music...

'They sustained this high through 'The Jack' and 'Highway To Hell' until halfway through 'Whole Lotta Rosie' they were unmanned by a farcical technical hitch... the entire PA was extinguished... unbeknown to the band, still deluged in onstage sound from monitors and back-line. Looking very silly they carried on screaming and stomping to themselves and must have been amazed to see the previously joyful crowd slow hand-clapping.

100

'Anyway, when normal service was resumed Angus and Bon went walkabout on the terraces with the radio guitar and they encored by demand with 'If You Want Blood...', which said it all for this earthy, honest, superb band.'

The Who? They were far too formulaic on this particular day, and their deliberated, studied mannerisms contrasted starkly with the genuine bonhomie and passion of Acca Dacca. It was most definitely a triumphant return to the UK for the band.

Following on from a string of festival appearances in Europe (which nearly culminated in a slot on the bill at the Reading Festival over August Bank Holiday weekend; however, that didn't quite come to fruition), AC/DC announced a full-blown UK tour, kicking off in Newcastle at the end of October, supported by Def Leppard. The trek lasted right through until December, with an incredible six-night run in two stints at the Hammersmith Odeon.

'Watching AC/DC in action is like inviting Blaster Bates round for tea and discovering that he uses gelignite to open the jam. You want blood? You've got it,' salivated Ian Ravendale when reporting in *Sounds* on the opening night of tour at the Newcastle Mayfair on October 26. The band should have also appeared the previous night at the same venue, but a fire at the Mayfair caused the postponement of the first date.

AC/DC ended the year by playing a date in Paris which was filmed for a long-form video issued in 1980 and titled 'Let There Be Rock'.

The next year began with a gig on January 25 at The Mayfair in Newcastle (replacing the show postponed from October 25) and a final date at The Gaumont in Southampton two days later, another concert that had to be rearranged from December when Bon sustained a leg injury. Support act for this brace of shows were Diamond Head, one of the fastest-rising British acts around.

January 27, 1980. AC/DC fans recall the date well. It was to be the last time Bon would appear onstage with the band. Less than a month later, he was dead...

CHAPTER EIGHT

DEATH OF A SUPREME SALESMAN

"Bon was one of the nicest guys I ever met. I really mean that. If he was an asshole I'd tell you. I'm not saying that just because the poor guy's dead. He really was a lovely guy... it was a great loss..."
– Ozzy Osbourne

In the early evening of Wednesday, February 20, 1980, Bon Scott was found dead in a car parked in Dulwich. The news, announced the following morning to a shocked media, sent AC/DC fans the world over into an immediate state of misery and depression that took years to lift – and in some cases still hasn't. What's more, the circumstances surrounding Bon's death were slightly hazy and remain something of a mystery, leading to all manner of wild speculation.

But let's concern ourselves with what is known. Bon had spent the first week of February in London, working on lyrics for the next album. He was even spotted at different times showing his hand-written lyrical ideas to various people he'd meet in pubs and clubs; in later months many were to allege that much of what was to become 'Back In Black' was written by Bon, even though he wasn't credited. This was never proven, though, and remains an unfounded claim. He also took time out to attend Angus' wedding to Ellen, his long-time Dutch girlfriend.

Things, so it seemed, couldn't have been better. Then on Tuesday, February 19, Bon went to tour manager Ian Jeffreys' house for dinner – a regular occurrence – leaving at about 6.30pm to go to the Music Machine, a venue in London now known as the Camden Palace. It was a regular haunt for Metal fans and musos. Bon was apparently supposed to meet UFO vocalist Phil Mogg and bassist Pete Way there, although neither actually showed up. But this would never have bothered Bon. He just held court, as was his wont, talking to all and sundry in a very good mood. When the club closed up its bar at 3am, Bon left with an old friend – someone who was later to give his name as Alisdair Kinnear.

Kinnear drove Bon back to his flat, but upon arrival found that the vocalist had passed out and was fast asleep. In fact, so deep was his sleep that Kinnear could not rouse him. What was he to do? Kinnear claimed that, unable to move Bon, the only thing he could do was to drive to his own flat in Dulwich in the hope that by the time he arrived there, Bon would wake up and could then crash out on his floor. But the hapless Kinnear was wrong in this assumption. When he arrived in Dulwich, Bon still refused to stir.

So Kinnear (who couldn't physically carry Scott out of the car and up to his flat) did the only thing that was open to him – or so he thought. He covered Bon with a blanket, locked the car and then crashed out himself – FOR 15 HOURS! Waking up in the early evening of February 20, Kinnear went down to his car, only to find that Bon still would not stir. By this time, Kinnear said he was beginning to panic and knew that this wasn't the simple result of a drunken binge. So, he drove Bon to Kings College Hospital, where tragically the singer was pronounced dead on arrival.

At the inquest held on Friday, February 23, the coroner delivered a verdict of 'death by misadventure'. At the inquest Kinnear, who described himself as a musician, told the court that Scott had drunk "at least seven double whiskies" at the Music Machine. But this

SOUNDS' OBITUARY FOR BON, 1980

AC/DC's Bon Scott: integral part of the band's macho persona.

(A touch too much)
Cruisin and boozin

behaviour wasn't exactly unusual for Bon. Surely, there must have been more to it than that.

And here's where rumour, innuendo and sensationalism began to set in. Word began to filter through that what had really caused Bon's death was heroin and not booze. He had been sold a bad batch of the hard drug, the story went, and this is what caused his death. Moreover, another name cropped up during enquires, namely one 'Joe King', who was also said to have been with Bon that night. 'King' was allegedly a drug dealer – but this name is said to be fictitious. Some even went so far as to speculate that AC/DC themselves were implicated in Bon's death! Obviously a blatant lie.

SOUNDS GIVES DETAILS OF BON'S FUNERAL, 1980

IOUXSIE: new single and t

Bon Scott flies home

AC/DC vocalist Bon Scott whose death due to alcoholic poisoning was announced in last week's issue, was buried in Perth, Western Australia last weekend. The rest of the band accompanied his body back home for the funeral, but they'll be returning to Britain this week when they'll be deciding on their next move.

They were originally planning to record their next studio album here and it's likely that they will, although no firm decision has yet been made. The position should become clearer within the next two weeks.

So what's the truth? Nobody is quite sure. There are gaps in the account, of that we can be certain. But we have been able to piece together something that does approach the definitive story.

'Joe King' is almost certainly a roadie who worked with various well-known Rock bands during the mid-'70s, and who was a friend of Bon's. There were rumours during this period that 'King' was involved with certain shady characters on the London scene (although it must be stressed this was never proven). It would seem that Bon met 'King' that fateful night before going to the Music Machine, possibly at the flat of his (Bon's) former girlfriend 'Silver' Smith, who at the time was struggling with drug addiction (from which she has since recovered). It is believed that at this point in the evening, Bon injected himself with supplied heroin, and then went down to the club where he met the innocent Kinnear. The rest followed as described.

Thus, Bon's death was a bizarre, tragic, yet ultimately accidental combination of circumstances. The reason so much of the story is shrouded to this day in mystery is simply because there were some rather unsavoury characters on the fringe who wanted to keep a safe distance between themselves and a high profile death of a Rock star. It worked. 'King' has since gone to ground, but as with so many charismatic stars who die in tragic circumstances, Bon's last hours continue to be the subject of much ill-informed speculation.

In *Sounds* on March 1, 1980, Dave Lewis (who knew the singer better than most) wrote a moving tribute to his lost friend:

'As a former roadie with the band who took over as vocalist after an impromptu (and very drunken) blow one night, he seemed to positively revel in the classic rock 'n' roll lifestyle. At 33 years of age, he was affectionately known as 'the old man' by the band's road crew, but in common with the rest of AC/DC he used to relish life on the road with its constantly changing scenery and cast – every night a different hotel and a different woman to take to bed (if he was lucky, and he usually was by all accounts).

'It was his escape route from the boredom of his smalltown Australian upbringing where the general attitude was that anyone who tried to make a living out of music was just a shirking lay-about, and probably a pooftah to boot.

'The thunderous thrashing of the AC/DC juggernaut inevitably meant that Bon Scott's voice was often virtually lost in the megawatt maelstrom and forced him to sing in a larynx-tearing screech for most of the time. Consequently, he was often singled out by reviewers as the weak link in the band – as just another Heavy Metal screamer, a criticism which was missing the point really.

'Bon was an integral part of the whole AC/DC persona, his gutsy, chest-beating vocals providing the ideal foil to the band's main weapon of attack – the non-stop broadside from Angus Young's

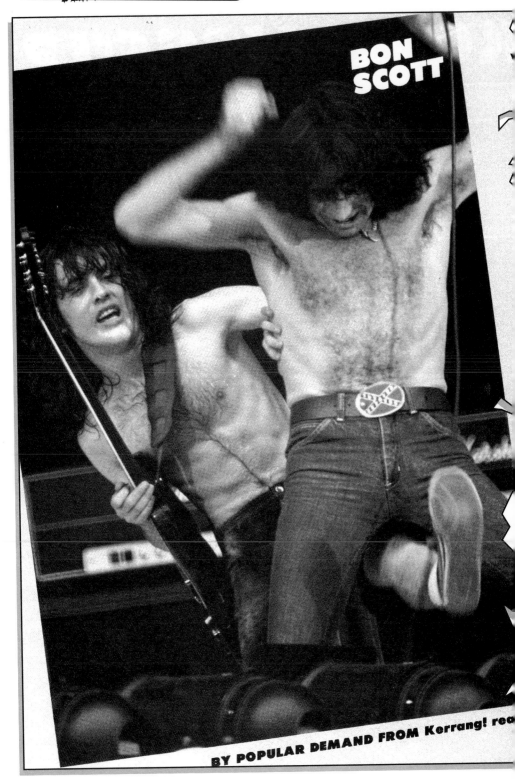

BON SCOTT

machine-gun guitar. While Bon strutted the stage and wailed his latest tale of drunken nights and hard-hearted women, Angus chugged up and down, whipping his sweat-soaked head from side to side in a powerchord world of his own. And though it was Angus who drove the hordes of young headbangers wild, it was Bon who the girls gawked at in his spray-on jeans, bare torso and lecherous grin, posing for all he was worth.

'My first memory of Bon Scott was at the Red Cow pub in Hammersmith during the Spring of '76 and the band's first-ever British visit when he amazed the packed crowd by carrying the guitar-flailing Angus out into the throng on his shoulders.

'With a Scots/Australian upbringing, Bon was hardly a great supporter of the equality of the sexes and his lyrics were littered with macho-man bravado, heightening his hard-drinking, hard-loving image. Yet strangely he was probably the least talkative in interviews – almost shy and retiring in comparison to the loquacious Angus. But when he was with the rest of the band, either onstage or in the bar, that was when he was in his element.

'As the apparent cause of his death indicates, Bon was a heavy drinker and had often been known to drink whole bottles of whisky during a single session, though I never saw him surly or aggressive no matter how much booze he had inside him. If after-gig exuberance led to a food-throwing fight or whatever, you could be sure Bon would be at the centre of the action, but he never sat back on his star status and was always happy to shake hands or sign autographs for fans – particularly if they were female.

'Basically, the phenomenal success of AC/DC opened up the doors for him to indulge in all the fun and games that his denim-clad legions of followers can only dream about. But, as Rock's grisly roll-call of terminal casualties proves only too well, it's a dangerous game to play, and sadly Bon went over the top once too often.'

The professionals weren't the only ones to pay homage to Bon's memory, as extracts from these letters to *Sounds* published on March 8 amply proved:

IN 1982, BON WAS STILL REVERED BY *KERRANG!* READERS

BON VOYAGE

IT WAS with great sorrow that I read in the paper about the death of Bon Scott.

The Reaper has taken one of the most talented, original rock singers around at this present moment. He will be sadly missed by me and many of my friends.

We know he was silly abusing his body with all that alcohol but you can't help feeling sorry for him. AC/DC has still got Angus Young, but Bon Scott was the vocalist, the communicator with the audience. Without him the magic is gone.

Let's hope AC/DC pull through this dilemma, but not in my wildest dreams can I imagine a vocalist to replace Bon Scott.

The magic is gone forever. Bon Scott is dead, long live Bon Scott. — Les Fisher, Monmouth, Gwent.

TRIBUTE TO BON SCOTT (RIP)

Bon, your life was magic
Your lyrics filled my head.
But your death was   tragic

And as I lie upon my bed
I reflect upon your music
I find it hard to see
How such a great musician
Could be so very mean
As to desolate the rock world
By doing a bunk, as such,
To that 'great gig in the sky'
By touching all too much.

No more to see you sing on stage
There's only your records left
So sad I am to see you die
Bon Scott, you were the best. — Phil, the cosmic Rush, Scorpions and AC/DC freak, Upton.

BON SHALL RETURN. 'For it is written in the book of Rock that he shall pass through the Highway To Hell and return in the Powerage with Blood And Balls and head for Sin City, where he shall smite the world with a good, hard, Kick In The Teeth. — Hawkfan, whose next best band are AC/DC, Dunde

EVEN
A LIF

A WEEK
to the Uria
Bradfor
minutes G
and we
had a fe
  A few m
came out a
would like
equipmen
we had g
the stage
told us to g
room to get
After we ha
autograp
finishe
  We fi
and we w
for a drink
and to
were
couple o
the roadie
talked wi
evening
would
concerne
Heep.
Leeds.

ONL
IS FA

SO WH
Def Le
been es
and are a
professio
F   bar
t   he
M
clin al a
Zeppelin
until the
'pop' tu
Rain' an
they en
isn't m
heavy r
Sabba
a cave
Waltha
  PS
as no
Zepp

I'M

110

'The Reaper has taken one of the most talented, original Rock singers around at this present moment. He will be sadly missed by me and many of my friends.'

'Bon Shall Return. For it is written in the book of Rock that he shall pass through the Highway To Hell and return in the Powerage with Blood and Balls and head for Sin City, where he shall smite the world with a good, hard Kick In The Teeth.'

But what of the remaining AC/DC quartet? Where did they stand? They quickly made it clear that there was no chance of giving up – no chance at all. They were enjoying the biggest success of their career, thanks to the 'Highway To Hell' album and also the just-released single 'Touch Too Much'. They would take time to get over the loss of Bon, but would certainly and determinedly forge on into the '80s.

Talking to Dave Lewis just a few short weeks after the tragedy, Angus explained how he heard about Bon's death. He told how he had received a panic phone call from Kinnear's landlady explaining how Bon had been rushed to King's College Hospital and declared dead on arrival...

"I immediately phoned Malcolm, cos at the time I thought maybe she's got the wrong idea, you know, thought it was him. And Ian (Jeffreys), our tour manager, said it couldn't be him cos he'd gone to bed early that night. Anyway, the girl gave me the hospital number, but they wouldn't give me any information until his family had been contacted. Anyhow, Malcolm rang Bon's parents cos we didn't want them to be just sitting there, and suddenly it comes on the TV news, you know.

"Peter (Mensch) our manager got to the hospital as soon as he could to find out exactly what had happened and identify him, because everyone was in doubt at the time. At first I didn't really believe it, but in the morning it finally dawned on me. It's just like losing a member of your family, that's the only way to describe it. Maybe even a bit worse, cos we all had a lot of respect for Bon as a person cos, even though he did like to drink and have a bit of a crazy time, he was always there when you needed him to do his job and things.

SOUNDS READERS' SORROW AT BON'S UNTIMELY DEATH, 1980

"I remember he missed a plane just once in Detroit (actually it was Phoenix) when he followed a girl that he'd met off the plane and ended up in some black ghetto – but that was typical of him, that was something we could laugh at. And he still got there the next day in time for the show. I think in his whole career there's maybe only three shows he's ever missed and that was cos his voice wasn't there and we didn't really want him to sing.

"Bon's parents were obviously in a bit of a shock about it and they had people from our record company in Australia there with them to look after all the details, but they never got the word about what really happened until we flew out there. That was really why we went, though we would've gone for the funeral, of course, but it was good to see them cos we'd met them a few times before and it was a bad thing for them, you know.

"It was a bad thing for us. I mean, as his Mum said, we spent more time with him than anyone. Bon joined us in '74 and had been with us ever since. There were even times when we had Christmases together.

"...I think it's more sad for the guy himself, you know, cos he always said he'd never go unless he was famous. And that's sad for him, because just as he was getting somewhere – cos he's been at it a lot longer than us, you know, he's been singing for something like 15 years – and it was sad for him in that way cos he really hadn't reached his peak.

"Malcolm and I were really looking forward to getting him in the studio and doing the next album; more than we've done with any album before because after the success of the last one, it was going to be a really big challenge, you know. That was the sad part of it, cos it could perhaps have been the best thing he'd ever done on record... That would've been the crowning glory of his life."

Angus also recalled Bon's character with affection during the same interview:

"Often he would trail off with fans who came backstage after a show and go off with them to a party or something. He judged people as they were and if they invited him somewhere and he was in the right mood to go, he went. It didn't matter to him whether they had a name or were a 'star', he just went with them. We used to call him

'Bon The Likeable'.

"We could be somewhere where you would never expect anyone to know him, and someone would walk up and say 'Bon Scott!' and always have a bottle of beer for him. It was uncanny.

"One time we were broken down in a bus outside this little town in Australia and some guy came walking along with his surfboard and a whole crate of beer. And it was really hot and we were dying for a drink. Anyway, he walked by the bus and looked in, saw Bon and suddenly yelled 'Bon Scott!' and came running in and handed out all his beers, and everyone was there for hours having a party while the bus was being fixed.

"He made a lot of friends everywhere and was always in contact with them too. Weeks before Christmas he would have piles of cards and things and he always wrote to everyone that he knew, keeping them informed. Even his enemies, I think.

"He certainly was a character."

Perhaps the finest testimony to the memory of Bon Scott – he was a character. A one-off. The blue collar hero who strode like a colossus through life, the bar, the boudoir, the recording studio and, ultimately, through history.

When he died, something of AC/DC died with him. He carried much of the band's spirit flowing freely in his veins. And it wasn't all booze. In fact, contrary to popular belief, Bon Scott wasn't an alcoholic. Whilst he could, in Angus' own words, "drink three bottles of bourbon straight off and he could drink like that constantly", he wasn't reliant on this level of intake. Indeed, close associates and friends have recalled that he could happily go for months without touching a drop of booze, if the mood so took him.

But there is no doubt that he left behind his own magnificent legacy in the form of a series of scorching albums that, to this day, remain peerless.

He also inspired tributes from other bands as well. American band Nantucket titled their next album 'It's A Long Way To The Top' and dedicated it to Bon, as did Canadian trio Santers with their album 'Shot Down In Flames'. Cheap Trick performed a version of 'Highway To Hell' in Paris during their 1980 European tour in Bon's honour.

WHOLE LOTTA BON

"All I can really say is that Bon is
and watching" — Brian

AC/DC were, and still are, a people's band
Scott a people's hero. Pure undiluted en
is what the band stand for, and Bon ep
this quality more than anyone. He took the musi
role in the band seriously, but never to the po
it estranged him from the fans. He en   ve
onstage and it showed.

His death in February 1980 (a freak ac
vomited when his neck was twisted a
marked the end of a six-year stint upfro
that time the band rose from a little-kn
playing sweaty gigs at the Red Cow. L
major force in the world of heavy ro
kuts like 'Highway To Hell', 'Bad B
and, above all, 'Whole Lotta Rosie
his own and, although 34 when
was still approaching his peak.

Clearly his death hit AC/DC ha
the suggestion of a fan in Chicag
singer Brian Johnson was we
the ranks and the band play
"I know that he approves
new line-up is trying to
Johnson, "He wo
wanted us to bu

French Metal punks Trust also dedicated their next album 'Repression' to the great man. Bon had been a friend and had agreed to translate their French lyrics into a form of English that was both accurate and also captured their innate sense of rage – a perfect choice for the job. Eventually Jimmy Pursey from Sham 69 inherited the job – and did it awfully.

Everywhere one turned in early 1980, Bon Scott's spectre seemed to dominate. But what of the band he had left behind? They were now faced with the near impossible task of carrying through their promise to find a replacement and soldier on. It was no easy task...

KERRANG! PAYS TRIBUTE TO BON IN 1982

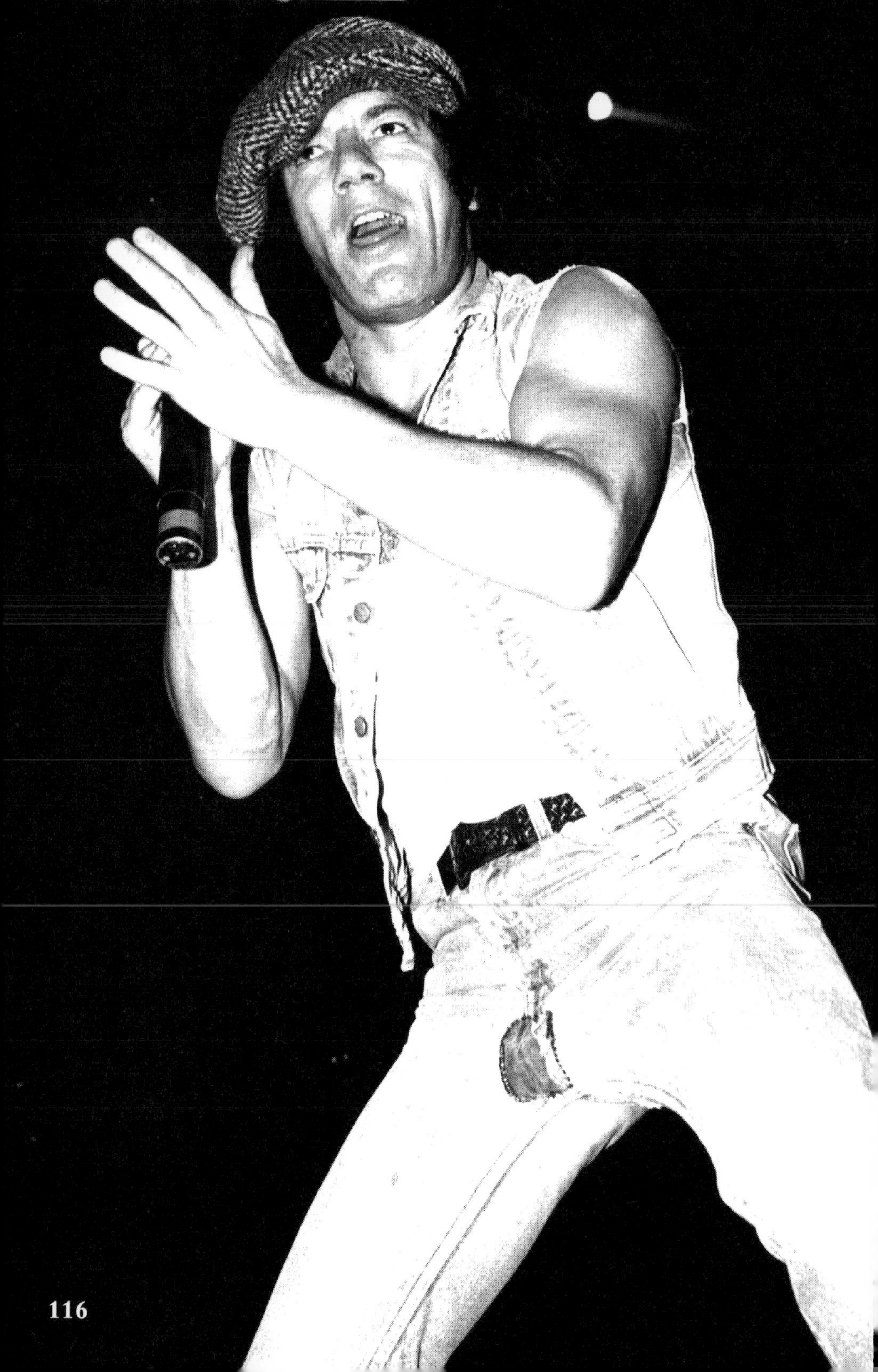

CHAPTER NINE

FEEL THE BLACK WIND

"When 'Back In Black' came out, everyone I knew had a copy and it was constantly played at parties. It was incredibly popular..."
– Jimmy Bowers (Crowbar)

"Everyone was walking around in silence. Nobody knew to do, we were so depressed. We were so close! It was like losing an arm." That was the way in which Angus summed up feelings in the AC/DC camp as they faced up to the enormity of the task now confronting them. How did they replace the irreplaceable and irrepressible Bon?

Inevitably, their departed vocalist dominated the band's thoughts until after the funeral. And, at that point, Malcolm and Angus pulled themselves together, and got down to the task of finding a new vocalist.

By the beginning of March, the media had lined up a number of likely candidates. Top of many people's list was ex-Easybeats man Stevie Wright. Why on earth he was courted remains a mystery. Wright had long since left the music business and was working for the Salvation Army back in Australia as a drugs counsellor! Perhaps it was the Vanda and Young connection that precipitated this ludicrous rumour. Maybe it was the notion that AC/DC themselves wanted a more mature singer to come into the fold and take over Bon's role.

Whatever, Wright's name was heavily touted – as indeed was that

117

AC/DC find new singer

AC/DC have found their replacement vocalist for Bon Scott. He's Brian Johnson who was formerly with Geordie, a Newcastle band who according to our silver haired honorary Geordie were "rampant Slade imitators". The band had two hits in 1974 — 'All Because Of You' and 'Can You Do It'.

The information came through just as *Sounds* was going to press and no further details were available.

AC/DC's first move is to complete the recording of their new studio album, which they were just about to start when Bon Scott died. Afterwards they'll be lining up an extensive touring schedule.

Brian Johnson will be talking to *Sounds* about his new job in next week's issue.

SOUNDS ANNOUNCE BRIAN
JOHNSON'S RECRUITMENT TO AC/DC, 1980

of Aussie Alan Fryer, who at the time was working in a band called Fat Lip, based in Adelaide. Fryer had a very similar personality to that of Bon – upbeat, vibrant, personable yet also possessing a certain rough charm and sweaty charisma. Maybe that was the problem with Alan: he was *too* similar to Bon. Putting him in the band would have immediately led to comparisons with his predecessor that would do AC/DC no good at all.

That Fryer could have done the job well, nobody who's met him would dispute. Just a few years later he joined Heaven, an Aussie band formed by Mark Evans (by now playing guitar) and managed by Michael Browning – both of whom are referred to in earlier chapters. The author spent one happy evening with Fryer in a New York restaurant, virtually drinking the place dry. There was little doubt that he could have walked into Acca Dacca and charmed everyone with his positivity and relaxed bonhomie. Apparently, Alan *was* seriously considered, but rejected.

Inevitably, the band were swamped with would-be replacements, most totally unsuitable and rejected as soon as their submitted tape hit the cassette player. But AC/DC persevered, and one of the more promising candidates was Londoner Gary Holton, a similar character to Bon with that blue collar sensibility that made the late Scott such an endearing man.

Holton had made his name in the '70s with the Heavy Metal Kids, and struck everyone who knew Bon as a logical choice. Everything about him smelled of myth and legend. There was even a story doing the rounds of how he'd angered some Hell's Angels one night in a pub. In revenge, Holton was allegedly kidnapped by the same Angels and forced to have sex all night long with a woman of their choice. If he failed to maintain his standards for the whole night, they threatened to kill him!

Legend has it that Holton duly obliged, and came through the 'ordeal' with flying colours – so much so that the Hell's Angels adopted him as form of mascot. Now that's a story Bon would have been proud to have doing the rounds about him!

**THE CLASSIC 'BACK IN
BLACK' LP, 1980**

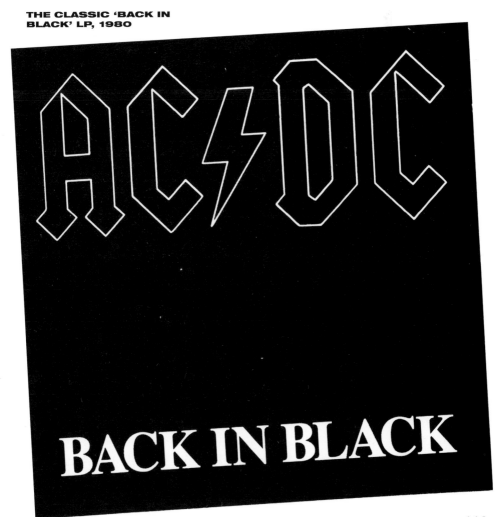

The problem with Holton, though, was that he had a serious booze problem. In fact, so bad was this situation that he was actually scheduled to audition for AC/DC down in a rehearsal studio hired by the band down in South London – but on three successive days, he failed to turn up! Holton's unreliability ruled him out of contention. He, of course, is best known these days for his role in successful comedy series 'Auf Wiedersehen Pet', still repeated at regular intervals. Sadly, he died in 1985. One can only speculate as to how Holton would have handled the challenge of stepping into Bon's shoes.

By the Spring of 1980, there was a shortlist of two vocalists: the veteran Terry Schlesser and one Brian 'Jonna' Johnson. The latter was very much the favoured choice by this time, and AC/DC spent a long time tracking him down to offer the chance of an audition. At first, the Tyneside warbler wasn't exactly bending over backwards to get the gig. He was busy trying to put his own band Geordie (successful during the early '70s) back together again. But he took time out to audition, running through just two numbers with Acca Dacca, namely their own 'Whole Lotta Rosie' and the Ike and Tina Turner monster 'Nutbush City Limits'.

Within a few days, Malcolm had called Brian up and told him he had the gig. Brian went out and celebrated in his native Newcastle, but nobody believed him. It was April 1!

So, just who was Brian Johnson? He was born on October 5, 1947 in Dunston, County Durham. He performed regularly in various different guises whilst a kid, even appearing in a TV play. But Brian was quickly bitten by the rock 'n' roll demon – and in February 1972 he joined the Newcastle band USA, also featuring guitarist Vic Malcolm, bassist Tom Hill and drummer Brian Gibson. They quickly changed their name to the more parochial Geordie. The band's first single, 'Don't Do That', was issued towards the end of the year through EMI, peaking at Number 32.

This was rapidly followed a few months later by their biggest hit in the form of 'All Because Of You', which reached Number Six in the charts, and another Top 20 hit with 'Can You Do It'. But the writing was very much on the wall for the stack-heeled foursome when their next single, 'Electric Lady', just scraped the lower reaches of the Top 40. Sadly, none of their albums – 'Hope You Like It' (1973), 'Don't

Be Fooled By The Name' (1974) and 'Save The World' (1976) – managed to persuade anyone to take the band seriously in the long-term. Shortly after the release of 'Save The World', Geordie called it quits.

Johnson actually gave up all hopes of making it in the music biz at this point. But by the beginning of 1980, he started to think about having another crack at the entertainment world. He persuaded his former colleagues to reform Geordie. At the time of the Acca Dacca approach, Geordie had just signed a deal with Red Bus Records in London, initially for a single ('Treat Her Like A Lady'/'Rockin' With The Boys'). Geordie elected to carry on when Johnson left, recruiting one Terry Schlesser as his replacement!

Any AC/DC completists who wish to have some Geordie in their collection should check out the compilation album 'Geordie Featuring Brian Johnson', released through Red Bus in January 1981. It features all the more popular tunes from the band, plus the aforementioned 'Treat Her...', never actually issued as a single.

Acca Dacca wasted no time in getting to work with 'Jonna'. They gave him a £5,000 signing-on fee plus a car, and flew him out to join them at Compass Point Studios in the Bahamas, where they were about to get to work on their latest album – again with 'Mutt' Lange at the helm.

But what was Johnson's perspective on his change in luck? Was he looking forward to the challenge of making this watershed album?

"Frankly, it scares the shit out of me," he told *Sounds'* Dave Lewis. "Cos some of AC/DC's most fanatical supporters come from Newcastle, and if any member of this band has so much as a bad tooth that lot would sense it. That's just the kind of fanatics they are up there.

"But if you try to understand the situation, I still don't know quite where I am, sitting here in the middle of London talking to you like this. All I know is there's a stack of work to do, and the rest of the band have still got to find out about me yet.

"Just coming down here (the band were at the time of this interview getting down to some serious rehearsing at E-Zee Studios in North London prior to heading for the Bahamas) and being with the lads is great, but I'm still scared shitless. Really, I'm talking about the future and that first gig and all those people waiting for the new album to come out – they're immediately going to make comparisons.

"But I suppose I'm a lucky lad in a way, cos I've never ever seen AC/DC play live or even on the TV. I've always been too busy gigging myself. I've heard all about 'em and their fantastic show, of course, and I've got all the albums in the house, cos it's my kind of music and I love 'em. I'm out-and-out basic, man, and to me they are one of the best rock 'n' roll bands in the world, doing things just to the basics, y'know.

"For me, you just canna whack rock 'n' roll, cos it dusna tell any lies, knorrimean? Anyway, at the moment, I'm just taking things bit by bit – cos they've got to learn how to do all the new songs too, you know. And I wudna mind splodging my doobries 'round Nassau for a

THE 'BACK IN BLACK' LINE-UP IN *SOUNDS*, 1980

, Brian Johnson hiding bald spot under convenient cap

Back with the bully boys

GEORDIE, WITH BRIAN JOHNSON, FAR LEFT

few weeks!

"The first time I met this lot, I really felt as if I could go out and have a pint with 'em and I wouldn't have to prove anything. Once you step inside their door and you meet these lads, the bullshit stops right on the doorstep. Everybody knows exactly what they're doing, from the manager right down to the road crew. And what I like is the way the lads treat the crew so well. And that crew, they'd die for those lads, you know.

"I think it's going to be great, me. It's going to be smashing once we've done one tour and people start saying, 'Okay, right, that's him, that's the new singer, he's the one now, so we've got to accept him'.

"Yeah, I'm going to be nervous at first, no doubt, but I'll give it my

123

AC/DC back in black

AC/DC have lined up a British tour for November — their first with new singer Brian Johnson.

The group are currently touring in America playing material from their new album 'Back In Black' which is released this weekend by Atlantic.

The tour starts on October 19 at Bristol Colston Hall and then continues at Leicester De Montfort Hall 20-21, Birmingham Odeon 22-23, Manchester Apollo 25-26, Sheffield City Hall 27-28, Hanley Victoria Hall 29, Glasgow Apollo November 1-2, Newcastle City Hall, Deeside Leisure Centre 6, Southampton Gaumont 7, London Hammersmith Odeon 10-12.

Tickets are priced at £4.50, £4.00 and £3.50 at all venues except Leicester, Deeside and Hanley which are all £4.50. The box offices open on July 24 except for Bristol which opens on August 7.

AC/DC's seventh album was recorded in the Bahamas with Mutt Lange producing

SOUNDS ANNOUNCE THE 'BACK IN BLACK' TOUR

best shot, you know. I mean, once I get up there I don't give a f**k, I just get on and do my best. But fortunately I've always been lucky enough to have a good rapport with audiences, so I just hope they give us a chance, you know."

Even at this early juncture, 'Jonna' insisted on being photographed with what has since become his trademark cloth cap firmly placed over his bonce (Lewis reckoned it was there 'because it keeps the sweat out of his eyes when he's onstage and he's grown attached to it. He is most definitely not doing an Elton John...') and his broad Geordie brogue has become as much a part of AC/DC tradition over the past 15 years as Angus' schoolboy uniform!

But back in the Spring of 1980, the world waited and watched – or at least, Acca Dacca fans did. Opinion was divided on whether this down-to-earth lad from Newcastle could replace the indefatigable Bon. But whoever had been chosen would have been greeted with equal measures of suspicion and goodwill. For, make no mistake there was goodwill towards the affable 'new bloke'. There might have been a certain trepidation among fans of the band, but there was an over-whelming hope that Johnson pulled it off.

The album, titled 'Back In Black' in Bon's memory, was complet-ed by the end of May. And on July 2, Johnson duly made his debut appearance onstage with the band at Arlon in Belgium. It went well – very well – with the crowd clearly showing they were on Johnson's side. What a boost that must have been!

"This kid came up to me when we did a warm-up show in Holland with a tattoo of Bon on his arm," 'Jonna' told *Sounds*. "He said, 'This bloke was my hero, but now he's gone. I wish you all the luck in the world'. I just stood there shaking. I mean, what can you say when people are prepared to put their faith in you like that? I hope I've been accepted by AC/DC fans."

On July 31, 'Back In Black' hit the streets. Within a couple of weeks, it was top of the UK charts! This was success of a magnitude few could have envisaged. And in November the album made it all the way to Number Four in the States. AC/DC were hot news!

Phil Sutcliffe in *Sounds* had no doubts about the album:

'In circumstances like this, the first album after the death of a favourite and crucial member of the band, it's easy to get confused about your reactions. But AC/DC, wild and reliable, have delivered again. That's the fundamental truth. The very slight hints on 'Highway To Hell' that they were Americanising – ie, softening their approach – have been elbowed aside... They continue to be the best Hard Rock band in the world, to my mind.

'At least five of the tracks have that adamantine toughness which I think they brought to 24-carat perfection a couple of years back with 'Hell Ain't A Bad Place To Be'. It's the solidity of Phil Rudd on drums and Cliff Williams on bass enhanced by the blood-empathy of the Young guitars. Their different energies dove-tail, the barmy fire of Angus and the sheer malice Malcolm gathers into his rhythm playing. They share a sense of timing and the power of the empty space around their megawatts.'

Sutcliffe was especially full of praise for the title track and album closer 'Rock And Roll Ain't Noise Pollution'. But what of Johnson's performance?

'Essentially, I just don't like him,' admitted Sutcliffe. 'It seems to me that in every respect, including appearance, the band's instincts led them against their better judgement to select the closest copy of Bon they could find... To put it into Deep Purple terms, I reckon that what AC/DC needed for a fresh approach was a bluesy David Coverdale. What they got was a screeching Gillan... I don't mean anything personal against Brian Johnson. I'm not saying he's a nasty chap and he's obviously tried very hard to fit the bill, but I think his assessment of AC/DC's needs were wrong. It's quite a tribute to the rest of them that 'Back In Black' remains a genuine, excellent AC/DC album.'

So less than total praise for the new boy, then? But in 1984, *Kerrang!*'s Mark Putterford was kinder to 'Jonna' on a re-assessment of 'Back In Black':

'His parrotesque vocals didn't seem a bit out of place as the new AC/DC rocketed back in style. The sombre black cover and the eerie chiming of a huge bell (apparently that was a struggle to get done; the first attempt was scuppered by the sound of birds chirping in the belfry!) seemed to mourn for Bon, but the band didn't dwell on nostalgia and presented a new-look AC/DC that coupled that ol' raunchy stomp with a touch of commerciality.

'I've grown to love the album... every song has individuality. From 'What Do You Do For Money Honey' and 'Let Me Put My Love Into You' to 'You Shook Me All Night Long' and 'Rock And Roll Ain't Noise Pollution', it's all classy, uplifting stuff.'

Nothing more need be added about this album, except to point out that Bon's inspiration hovered over much of the lyrical content. Indeed, several close associates of Bon's maintain to this day that, whilst he wasn't credited for penning any lyrics on this album, nonetheless they had actually been shown some of the lines used on the album by Bon himself – written in his own hand! This, of course, could never be proven and remains no more than conjecture, about which the author remains cynical.

Did AC/DC diplomatically credit their new boy in order to bolster his confidence? All that one can say is that, at the time Dave Lewis introduced 'Jonna' to the world through the pages of *Sounds* whilst the band were rehearsing for the album, it seemed evident from what was said that the new singer had not had time to make any contribution to the lyrical content of the record (wrote Lewis in the April 19 edition of *Sounds*: 'Also, although he's hopeful of eventually lending his songwriting talents to the AC/DC machine, he's in no great hurry'). What the hell? 'Back In Black' was still a fitting tribute to Bon – and also a magnificent way in which to introduce a whole new era for the band. Johnson did himself and the band proud.

On July 30, the band began their massive US tour in Eerie, Pennsylvania. They were now major stars in America. By the time Dave Lewis reported on the tour for *Sounds*, the band were unstoppable – the biggest name in America at the time.

'AC/DC are currently more than two months into their taking-America-by-storm tour,' said Lewis from the Long Beach Arena in California. 'Their audiences have doubled since their last visit and you can barely turn the radio on without hearing one of their songs... Just about everything about this band at the moment screams SUCCESS.'

BACKSTAGE PASS FOR THE 1980 'BACK IN BLACK' TOUR

Lewis also found them unchanged as people.

'Though AC/DC are very definitely Big Time these days, there is none of the preening, posing Rock star ego in these boys. They may be staying at the semi-legendary Sunset Marquis Hotel (in West Hollywood) where Bruce Springsteen can be seen wandering around in the lobby, but Brian Johnson still insists on cooking his own English-style eggs and bacon for breakfast... And their idea of a good time is a few games of darts in the small bar, dubbed Hell's Kitchen, that the roadies have set up at the side of Angus Young's onstage cat-walk (this was the band's haven from the excesses and glamour of stardom, and membership of this exclusive bar had to be purchased!).'

The show Lewis witnessed was spectacular:

'A deafening roar and a fusillade of fire crackers greets the dimming of the arena's lights, and the sound of a tolling bell booms out of the towering speakers. Slowly, the curtains open to reveal AC/DC's recently acquired extravagance, a huge, bronze church bell (cast in Loughborough, England) being lowered towards the stage, where Brian waits to clobber it with a big wooden mallet.

'AC/DC live are an experience never to be forgotten; their thundering, rolling Rock grabs you by the ears, while Angus' onstage antics poke you straight in the eye. For just a moment, I felt a strange twinge of shock on seeing not Bon Scott but Brian up there with the mike, but it lasted a few seconds and the truth is that AC/DC are as strong now as they ever were.'

The seal of approval.

"It's good to feel that we've kept going and things are finally starting to happen, instead of feeling we were battering our heads against a brick wall," Angus told Lewis after the show. "It was a great thrill when the album went to Number One in the UK. I just couldn't believe it when I got the call. Thanks, England. To me that means more than anything happening here in the States, because I've always regarded Britain as a credible place, much more so than America or anywhere else."

"To me now, it's just frightening how big this band are going to become in the next three or four years," added 'Jonna'. "I have said right from the start with AC/DC that I need everybody to please just give me a year to fit in, because it's such a big change in the band obviously. Once this tour of America is over, I've got to cross the same bridge in Britain..."

That 'bridge' was crossed during October, when the band debuted at the Colston Hall in Bristol on the 19th. It was a massive tour, lasting until November 16 (including six dates in London – three at the Hammersmith Odeon, three more at the Apollo in Victoria). How were they received? Over to Pete Makowski's views, as printed in *Sounds* on November 22:

'It goes without saying that the place was packed. These guys could probably do a month's residency at the Odeon, no problem. AC/DC are a well-oiled machine, professional to the hilt, and even though they're in the final weeks of one of their monster tours and probably totally shagged out, they still manage to play each night like it's the first. Brian Johnson fits in like a glove. There's no way anyone could emulate Bon as his basic asset was sheer personality, the vocals were just an extension... Johnson has equal street cred, but takes a more professional approach to his craft. He comes from a tradition of powerhouse vocalists, and although he wears a flat cap and looks like one of the geezers from your local, he knows how to pose and is aware of his vocal capacity.

'To be quite honest, that night his voice (compared by Makowski to Robert Plant and Nazareth's Dan McCafferty) sounded shot, but he still put on a brave face and didn't let the side down. My criticisms were aimed mainly at Angus, who at times is over-indulgent on his soloing, which without the leaping about and lunacy would sound no more inspiring than a second-rate Alvin Lee – although within the context of a song, his playing is short, sharp and straight to the point.

'Like, say, Status Quo, an AC/DC show is the closest musical equivalent to a football match... The audience identify with each other. They have one common love – AC/DC... One of the top five live acts around.'

Acca Dacca finished the year with a triumphant homecoming to Australia, following on from a spectacularly successful tour of Japan. The band were now a worldwide phenomenon.

Taking a welcome break after all of this action, AC/DC could take stock of their immensity as 1981 dawned: 'Back In Black' was on its way to selling 10 million copies in the States alone. The chart-topping album had generated two Top 40 singles in the UK, namely 'You Shook Me All Night Long' and 'Rock And Roll Ain't Noise Pollution'.

AC/DC had arrived on the very biggest of stages. And they kept going on the road during the early part of '81, heading out once again for a US tour. In May, 'Dirty Deeds Done Dirt Cheap' finally gained a US release, reaching Number Three.

AC/DC's fame did stir up some unwelcome attention, though,

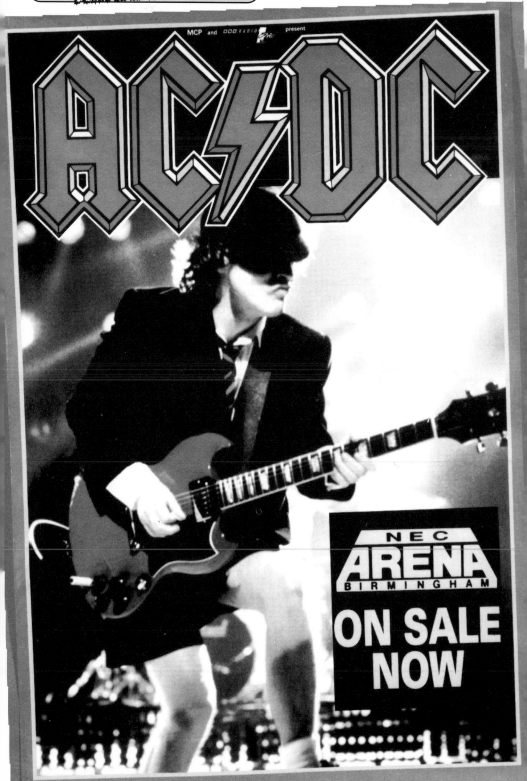

when a couple in Libertyville, Illinois sued them for $250,000, claiming that the band had given out their phone number on the title track from 'Dirty Deeds...', and were therefore responsible for an alleged string of obscene calls they'd received. The couple's number was 362 436, which was mentioned by Bon in the lyrics *('Call me any time/36 24 36/I lead a life of crime')*, but this was pure coincidence.

"The numbers are simply my dream girl's vital statistics," Angus told *Sounds*. "I thought any red-blooded male would realise that." How Bon would have smirked at this episode.

The US tour proved to be both tiring yet exhilarating. And in June the band received a significant reminder of their huge, unparalleled UK popularity when the very first issue of *Kerrang!* (with Angus on the cover) saw readers of *Sounds* (*Kerrang!* started life as a spin-off from the latter) vote 'Whole Lotta Rosie' the greatest Heavy Metal track of all time. So, howzabout a British date to celebrate?! No problem...

CHAPTER TEN

WE, MONSTERS!

"Brian Johnson is one of the funniest men I've ever met. He's just hilarious, always telling jokes. I've often told him that he should record an album of his jokes!"

– Klaus Meine (Scorpions)

On August 22, 1981, AC/DC received the final confirmation – if any were needed – that they were now one of the very biggest Rock bands in the world. The quintet were offered the chance to headline the second annual Castle Donington Monsters Of Rock binge. This was really the birth of the festival *per se*. Sure, the year previously, Rainbow had topped the bill at the very first Monsters Of Rock – but that had actually been more of a Rainbow gig than a true festival.

When Acca Dacca were approached to appear in '81, it really was the start of what has become arguably the most famous Heavy Metal festival in the world.

For the band, of course, it wasn't their first outdoor appearance in the UK. In '79, they'd played with The Who at Wembley Stadium (as previously discussed). And in 1980, *Sounds* had linked them with a proposed festival at the Crystal Palace Bowl, with Judas Priest the rumoured headliners and America's wild man Ted Nugent also likely to be on the bill. Sadly, this all came to nothing. By the time Donington '81 came around, AC/DC were the most logical of choices to headline.

Joining them on the bill were Whitesnake (fronted by ex-Deep Purple man David Coverdale), American legends Blue Öyster Cult and Blackfoot, Slade (who were hotly tipped to be the biggest success of the day, having taken the Reading Festival by storm the previous year) and young English hopefuls More. For Acca Dacca, Donington came as they were preparing to record a new album. But it also came a something of a welcome relief for them, because there were problems with the record.

The band had spent three weeks during July and August rehearsing in a huge, abandoned factory on the outskirts of Paris. But once in the studio, 'Mutt' Lange simply couldn't get the sound right. When Acca Dacca left for Donington, it was with a certain sense of irritation. There was still much work to be done on the record.

Donington provided a welcome breath of fresh air. More than 60,000 fans braved awful weather to celebrate the day's action. But not everything went according to plan. For, as the lights went down and the band prepared to take to the stage... well, this is how Brian Johnson described what happened to *Sounds*:

"The crowd were cheering like mad, but as we were going up the steps to the stage, some security guy says to Malcolm, 'Come on, get off - you haven't got a pass!'. So I said, 'Oi, he's in the band!' and the guy says, 'And you can shut up – you ain't coming up here either!'."

Just another day in the 'office' for the lads! Fortunately, the confusion was soon sorted out and the band gave their all in a welter of lights and sweat. Most fans believed that AC/DC were well worth the entrance money, even if they were given a real run for their money by Whitesnake (delivering arguably their finest performance to date) and Slade, who were one of the best live bands of all time.

Perhaps the silliest thing to happen at the festival involved not Acca Dacca but Blue Öyster Cult. Just a few days prior to the festival, the band suffered a massive blow when drummer Albert Bouchard walked out. In order to fulfil their commitment to Donington, the band had to draft in drum roadie Rick Downey as his replacement. They went onstage at the festival fearing the worst – and it happened! They were an unmitigated disaster.

Later, backstage, the band were presented with commemorative plaques, but so irate was guitarist/vocalist Eric Bloom at events that he threw the plaque onto the grass and jumped up and down on it! A perfect summation of what had been an awful day for BÖC...

Bloom, though, wasn't the only one having a problem. Donington promoter Maurice Jones was walking around during this great day on crutches! The reason? Just a couple of weeks previously, Maurice had hosted a party at his house following Whitesnake's show at the nearby Stafford Bingley Hall. The whole of AC/DC had turned up and proceeded to enjoy the hospitality on offer – including assorted alcoholic beverages.

Sadly, Malcolm Young became rather too playful with Maurice, and as a joke pushed him into a pond! Unfortunately for the hapless promoter, one of his feet became wedged in some rocks – and in the ensuing *melée*, he broke his ankle!

But even this couldn't dampen Maurice Jones' great personal pride at this occasion. He and his company MCP had been AC/DC's promoters since their arrival in the UK. Now, to see all his

BACKSTAGE PASS FOR DONINGTON MONSTERS OF ROCK, '81

belief and hard work paying off in such spectacular fashion was very emotional – if a little painful.

So well had AC/DC's appearance gone in 1981 that it came as no surprise to see 'em again in the frame for the festival three years later. Neither Status Quo (1982) nor Whitesnake (1983) had proved to be as big a draw as the Aussie legends. First news of this appearance came in *Kerrang!* towards the end of March, when it was confirmed that Angus, Malcolm and the lads would indeed top the bill. Tickets were to be priced at a bargain £11, and the event would take place on August 18. But who else would appear? Initial rumours suggested that

Van Halen, Kiss and Krokus were all in the frame – and within a week VH were announced as the special guests.

The rest of the bill slowly came to light, being finalised as follows: AC/DC, Van Halen, Ozzy Osbourne, Gary Moore, Y&T, Accept and Mötley Crüe.

'It wasn't until I strolled into the arena that I realised the full implications of this year's Monsters Of Rock Festival,' wrote Derek Oliver at the start of *Kerrang!*'s enormously detailed review of Donington '84. 'The sheer outrageous size of everything in view, from the massive PA stacks to the unending sea of pale blue denim ,was simply staggering.'

This, indeed, was to prove arguably Donington's finest day. The weather was mag-

POSTER ADVERTISING DONINGTON '81

AC/DC

ANGUS YOUNG

nificent (sun, sun... and more sun). The attendance was enormous (some 80,000-plus) and the music... oh, the MUSIC!

Openers Mötley Crüe came onstage at 12 noon – 30 minutes earlier than expected. 'Greeted initially with a little apprehension,' wrote Oliver, 'including some familiar missile throwing, they rose to the challenge in fighting fashion and won the crowd's affection within the space of their first number, the appropriately titled 'Bastard'.'

Mötley were a triumphant opening band, even if bassist Nikki Sixx climaxed their set by throwing his bass into the audience and hitting an unsuspecting fan on the head!

Germans Accept received a rave review from Mick Wall: 'They were the best band I saw all day. Udo and the boyz came top of the poll for guts, energy and, best of all, loudness!'

Mark Putterford, though, wasn't totally overwhelmed by San Francisco's Y&T: 'The band lack one vital ingredient which'd make 'em outstanding. After their Donington performance I couldn't put my finger on the missing factor, continuing to regard the boys as merely a good band of no special attraction... Sadly, the biggest hit of their performance was the bottle that caught (mainman) Dave Meniketti full on the mush.'

Gary Moore, in contrast, delivered just what was expected, according to Wall: 'He paraded his talents with assurance and the natural aplomb of the true Guitar Hero.'

As for Ozzy Osbourne? 'He stole the show,' raved Oliver. 'Rolling around in a cradle of animalistic riffs, he crushed his festival contemporaries with the delicacy of King Kong buggering a defenceless field mouse... Simply the greatest.'

Van Halen, though, were the band many were looking forward to watching at the festival. So how did they perform? According to the *Kerrang!* review, they were less than impressive. It was claimed that the set wasn't worth the wait, that in overall terms, VH's show had to be construed as a disappointment.

And so to Acca Dacca, the band everyone was waiting for. But again, the *Kerrang!* review was less than ecstatic. The claim was made

KERRANG! CAPTURES ANGUS IN ACTION AT DONINGTON, 1984

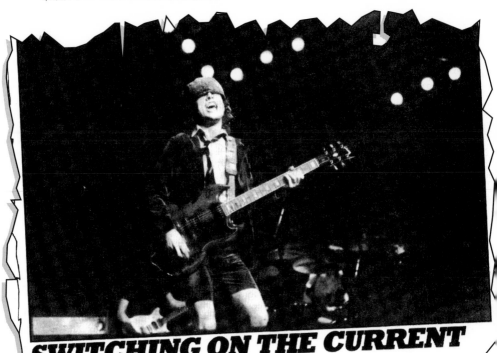

SWITCHING ON THE CURRENT

■ *AC/DC (GUITARIST* **Angus Young** *pictured above) are to headline the fifth annual Castle Donington Monsters of Rock Festival, to be held on August 18. This will be the band's only UK show during 1984.*

As yet no other band has been confirmed for the bill and a spokesman for promotors Wooltare has stated that: "Recent suggestions concerning **Van Halen**

Krokus *and* **Kiss** *appearing at the festival are no more than pure speculation".*

Tickets for Donington cost £11 and are available by postal application only from: **Wooltare Ltd, PO BOX 123, Walsall, West Midlands.** *An SAE should be enclosed and all cheques/postal orders should be made payable to* **'Wooltare Ltd'.** *Overseas applicants should send an international*

money order to include coverage all postal charges, as well as an unstamped self-addressed envelope. All members of AC/DC's official fan club should note that special ticket arrangements are being made for them. A letter from the club will be sent out imminent outlining these plans.

Tickets will also be available on the day of the gig at the festival site priced at £12.

KERRANG! ANNOUNCES DONINGTON '84

that AC/DC were better when they were more of a Punk band. Moreover, it was stated that since Bon Scott's sad death, they've been on a downhill slope.

The review went on to pontificate that now the band were virtually a dinosaur, and that what was wrong with AC/DC's performance at Donington was that it lacked heart. Sure, it was admitted, they played well; it was a good show, and everybody onstage and in the crowd had looked as if they were having fun. But it just wasn't the same as the good old days, when the band played in pubs before hundreds, rather than at festivals before tens of thousands.

So, was this the start of the media's backlash against the thus-far impregnable band? No chance. The fans were still sticking by their heroes. A week after the above review of Acca Dacca appeared in *Kerrang!*, an anonymous AC/DC fan wrote this letter to the magazine:

'AC/DC are one of the hardest, if not *the* hardest, working bands in the world; just because they aren't always playing in the UK doesn't mean that they've sold out to the US and have kicked us Brits in the teeth, unlike some US bands, ie Van Halen... No, AC/DC have proven that by sticking to good old traditional rock 'n' roll (no synths here!), it's possible to stay at the top – as they proved at Castle Donington this year. Thanks to Angus and Co for a great evening.'

The event marked the live debut of new drummer Simon Wright – at least in the UK (more about this situation in a later chapter), and most observers believed that, whilst Van Halen had certainly been popular with audience (they were then, of course, at the height of their commercial appeal, thanks to the hit single 'Jump' and the album '1984'), it was AC/DC who came out on top.

This wasn't for the want of trying on the part of VH vocalist David Lee Roth. He did his best in the run-up to Donington to claim that Van Halen would blow the Aussies off the stage. He even went so far as to stage a supposedly impromptu (but actually well planned) demonstration of aerobics in his own backstage area – which just happened to coincide with an AC/DC photo call. And did this and his blaring personal hi-fi system (which was almost as big as the Donington PA!) and ostentatious posturing distract the assembled snappers? Just a bit!

AC/DC's reaction to all of this wasn't recorded at the time; one can only speculate as to whether they were amused or angry. Whatever, their no-nonsense brand of pure Hard Rock, with few frills but considerable torrents of energy, was good enough to receive rapturous applause from the masses – who might have been enthralled with Van Halen's Americanised glamour, but still preferred the down-to-earth honesty of their long-time heroes.

Perhaps one of the reasons why the media seemed so hooked on Van Halen instead of praising Acca Dacca was because the latter's profile had dropped considerably in the weeks leading up to that

Monsters Of Rock. The band refused to do interviews or photo sessions to promote their appearance or the festival in general, whilst David Lee Roth and the rest of the VH cavalcade were only too delighted to get involved with the press in order to push their return to the UK.

Perhaps the novelty of an AC/DC festival extravaganza had worn off. You got what you expected – no more, no less. But the fans understood and continued to hail them as true megastars of the genre.

Seven years later, AC/DC set a new record by becoming the first (and thus far only) band to headline the festival on three occasions! Rumours started to spread that this would be the case as early as January 1991. And in the April 20 edition of *Kerrang!* that year, the full line-up of bands for the festival (set to be held on August 17) was confirmed: AC/DC (with yet another new drummer in tow – this time Chris Slade), Metallica, Mötley Crüe, Queensrÿche and the Black Crowes. Tickets had by this time gone up in price to £22.50.

The week of the festival itself, *Kerrang!* scribe Paul Elliott spoke to Angus Young, who admitted:

"People have said we've hung around long enough! Some bands fade when they try to adapt to what's current. We play Rock music. It's a little too late for us to do a ballad. Rock is what we do best. Sometimes I'm asked if I want to play music other than AC/DC. Sure, at home I play a little Blues – but after five minutes I'm like, 'Sod this!' and I'm playing Hard Rock again.

"Sometimes it is frightening (to play before a huge Donington-style audience), yeah, but you gotta psyche yourself up a bit, give yourself a good kick up the ass. Being older, Malcolm's the best person to give me a kick. He'll just say to me, 'Those feet look a little slow tonight'. Usually, once I've got the uniform on I'm okay. I'm on edge, nervous, but I'm not in a panic. At least I don't have to put on make-up. I sport my own pimples!

"I think the first time I wore the uniform was the most frightened I've ever been onstage... (usually) adrenalin takes over. It's like when you take off in an aeroplane. It's exhilarating. When you're firing

POSTER ADVERTISING THE CLASSIC DONINGTON '84 LINE-UP

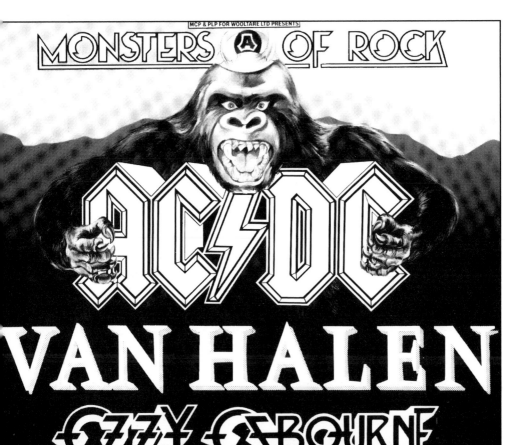

MCP & PLP FOR WOOLFARE LTD PRESENTS

MONSTERS OF ROCK

AC/DC

VAN HALEN

OZZY OSBOURNE

GARY MOORE

Y&T

Accept · MÖTLEY CRÜE

TOMMY VANCE

DONINGTON PARK
SATURDAY 18th AUGUST 1984

TICKETS £11.00 ADVANCE (subject to booking fee) AVAILABLE FROM:

AC/DC'S DRESSING ROOM AREA, DONINGTON '84

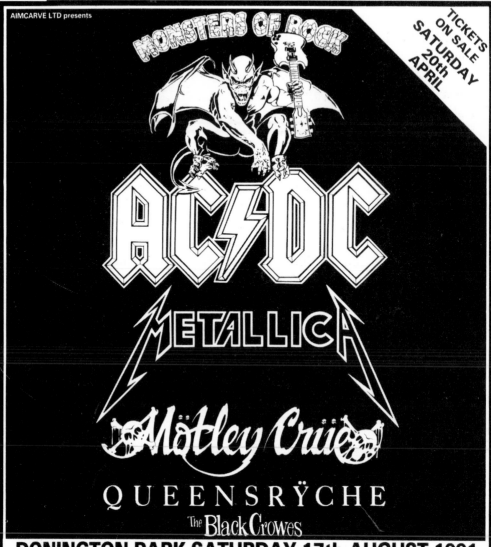

AIMCARVE LTD presents

MONSTERS OF ROCK

TICKETS
ON SALE
SATURDAY
20th
APRIL

AC/DC
METALLICA
Mötley Crüe
QUEENSRŸCHE
The Black Crowes

DONINGTON PARK SATURDAY 17th AUGUST 1991

Tickets: **£22.50 (inc. VAT)** Subject to a booking fee *Gates open 10.30 am - First Band 2.00 pm*

ADVANCE TICKETS ONLY - NO TICKETS WILL BE SOLD ON THE DAY

TICKETS ARE AVAILABLE FROM:-
ABERDEEN: One-Up
BELFAST: Harrison Musique
BIRMINGHAM: Odeon Theatre
BIRMINGHAM: Ticket Shop
BIRMINGHAM: Way Ahead
BLACKBURN: King Georges Hall
BRADFORD: St. Georges Hall
BRIGHTON: Brighton Centre
BRISTOL: Our Price
CAMBRIDGE: Millers Music Centre
CARDIFF: City Centre Ticketline

COVENTRY: Poster Place
DERBY: Way Ahead
DUBLIN: Ticketshop at HMV
DUNDEE: Groucho's
EDINBURGH: Playhouse Theatre,
EDINBURGH: Virgin Records
GLASGOW: Just the Ticket (TOCTA)
GLOUCESTER: Gloucester Leisure Centre
HANLEY: Mike Lloyd Music
HULL: Gough & Davy
LEEDS: Cavendish Travel

LEICESTER: De Montfort Hall
LINCOLN: Way Ahead
LIVERPOOL: Royal Court Theatre
LONDON: Hammersmith Odeon
LONDON: LTB
LONDON: Stargreen Box Office
LONDON: Keith Prowse & Co. Ltd.
LONDON: Premier Box Office Ltd.
LONDON: Albemarle Booking Agency
LONDON: Ticketmaster
MANCHESTER: Apollo Theatre
MANCHESTER: Piccadilly Records

NEWCASTLE UNDER LYME: Mike Lloyd Music
NEWCASTLE UPON TYNE: City Hall
NEWPORT: Newport Centre
NOTTINGHAM: Way Ahead
OXFORD: Apollo Theatre
POOLE: Arts Centre
PORTSMOUTH: Guildhall
READING: Hexagon
SHEFFIELD: City Hall
STAFFORD: Lotus Records
WOLVERHAMPTON: Mike Lloyd Music

COACH OPERATORS
South West, Wales, South Coast, Avon, Cotswolds & Swindon:
The Concert Travel Company 0271 74447
East Anglia: Steve Jason Concert Travel 0733 60075
Scotland: Show Travel 0382 561133
North East England: Cavendish Travel 0532 441919/0742 754774 or Selbys Travel 0482 227434
Humberside: Selbys Travel 0482 227434
East & West Midlands: Rock Trips 0602 414212
London: Rock Trips 071-434 1363
Yorkshire: Cavendish Travel 0532 441919 or Rock Trips 0602 414212/0602 483456
North West England: Argon Events 0942 896868
South East: Furlongs 0732 741066

POSTAL APPLICATION
Tickets are available from Aimcarve Ltd., PO Box 123, Walsall WS1 2NY. Enclose postal order or cheque made payable to Aimcarve Ltd. and send SAE. Tickets £22.50 (inc. VAT) plus 50p booking fee per ticket. (People sending cheques should allow 21 days for clearance).

PLEASE NOTE
No bottles or cans of any description will be allowed onto the site, if you want to bring liquid refreshments use ½ gallon or 1 gallon square cordial type containers - round containers are not acceptable.
Anyone found throwing any object will be charged by the Police with Public Disorder.

IMPORTANT
The only official merchandise is on sale inside the festival site. Please do not buy anything outside.

CREDIT CARD APPLICATIONS Tel: 0602 483456 or 0602 414212 (Subject to an administration fee of £2.00 per ticket).

well, it's the best feeling in the world. When it goes wrong, it's like someone's shoved a red hot poker up yer backside!

"Cos of nerves, I've tripped and even forgotten to do my zipper up a few times! I go for a pee and forget. Last thing before I go onstage, I always go for a piss and then have a cigarette. If you ever see my shorts smoking, you know I didn't put it out right!

"(After a show) I just wind down for a couple of hours. I try to hide, just in case somebody grabs me and says, 'Hey, you didn't play this song tonight!'. We don't get much rest on the road, with days running into the next. I need time to relax. I wouldn't like to be Angus-Young-onstage all the time. I'd be burnt out inside a week."

So, what of the festival itself? The Black Crowes opened up the proceedings, but frankly didn't take the crowd by storm. 'The Crowes are brilliant, but today they're misguided and misplaced... Nope, the Black Crowes definitely ain't Donington-type dudes.'

The Crowes were followed by Queensrÿche, who again didn't exactlty receive a full thumbs-up on the day from *K!* reviewer Xavier Russell: 'I know I'm in a minority when I say I prefer the Queensrÿche of yesteryear. I wasn't totally alone in thinking this either – a kouple of 'eadbangers behind me kontinually kried for 'The Lady Wore Black'. Natch, it wasn't played and we went home disappointed.'

But Mötley Crüe fared rather better, at least in the eyes of the *K!*'s Ray Zell: 'For Donington '91, Mötley Crüe were the sun invadin' a black alley an' a pile o' shit on a sandy beach. A necessary imperfection.'

Metallica also got the nod of approval from Don Kaye in the hallowed pages: 'Yes, I've seen tighter performances, but I've seen a lot more sterile acts as well. Metallica's sheer power and lurking sense of fun carry them over any rough spots. The masters are back, in triumph.'

But this was very much AC/DC's day – as usual at the Monsters Of Rock! Let's leave it to *K!*'s writer on the spot, Chris Watts, to give his

POSTER ADVERTISING DONINGTON 1991

147

opinions on the headliners:

'AC/DC are 'stable' in the truest sense of the word. They have not strayed from their chosen path in 15 years. Hell, they haven't even edged sideways in some peculiar attempt to keep abreast of their peers. AC/DC simply exist, and they are absolutely incapable of being crap.

'So the police are singing the praises of the Donington crowd at 5.30pm on the BBC news. Certainly, there was not much approaching a riot, but the response to the surreal vision of a giant blow-up doll hanging over AC/DC during 'Whole Lotta Rosie' must have come close. There ain't much you can do to top one of Metal's all-time classics, but the doll was daft and cool, nonetheless. AC/DC's little joke.

'Of course, you can argue as to whether AC/DC should actually have been asked back to headline Donington for the third time, but you cannot argue that AC/DC went down a storm. They cannot fail to top a festival in style. You just know it from the opening blast of 'Thunderstruck' and the first glimpse of Angus Young up there on the catwalk... Beside him, Brian Johnson is probably what they still call workmanlike. A stout, leather-faced old pro with his lungs and leer intact after all these years of screeching and growling and leching and rasping...

'AC/DC's set is, well, you know... comfortable. Their unshakable strength is several tank-busting songs and a no-frills delivery that will never let them down. Really, AC/DC are that simple... They just cannot fail with 'Let There Be Rock', 'Whole Lotta Rosie' and 'Highway To Hell' to bring the set to a close. No chat, no bullshit and no girlie singalongs... They still look dead chuffed that we remember all the words.

'Natch, the 21-cannon salute to close both the encore of 'For Those About To Rock (We Salute You)' and Castle Donington '91 makes like the Royal Tournament. As ever, it's a punter-friendly gesture that once again seals a surefire victory. AC/DC – from the top of Chris Slade's immaculately bald pate to the bottom of Malcolm

COVER FOR *KERRANG!*'S COVERAGE OF DONINGTON '91

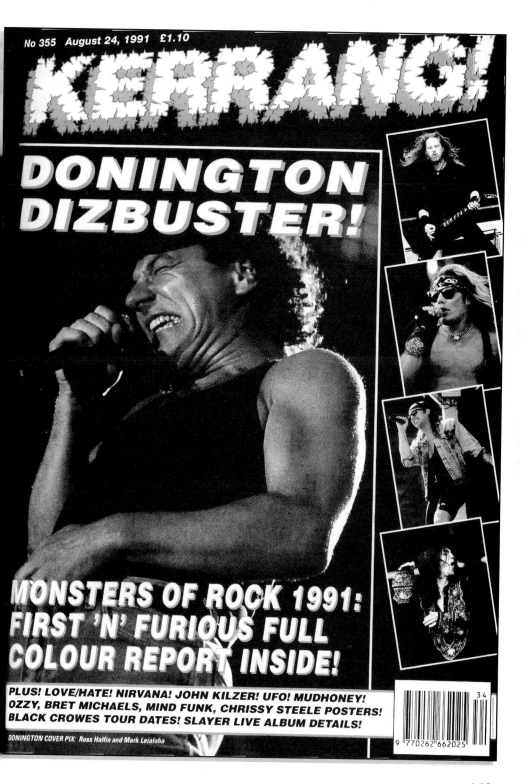

No 355   August 24, 1991   £1.10

KERRANG!

DONINGTON DIZBUSTER!

MONSTERS OF ROCK 1991: FIRST 'N' FURIOUS FULL COLOUR REPORT INSIDE!

PLUS! LOVE/HATE! NIRVANA! JOHN KILZER! UFO! MUDHONEY! OZZY, BRET MICHAELS, MIND FUNK, CHRISSY STEELE POSTERS! BLACK CROWES TOUR DATES! SLAYER LIVE ALBUM DETAILS!

DONINGTON COVER PIX: Ross Halfin and Mark Leialoha

9 770262 662025

KERRANG!

DONINGTON 1991
12 PAGE PULL-OUT PREVIEW SPECTACULAR

INCLUDES
OFFICIAL
EVENT
POSTER!

ANGUS YOUNG of AC/DC: pic Ray Palmer

Young's dreadful teeth – are the oldest young men in town. The global bar band, and irreplacable.'

What more can be said? Another triumph for the band – yet more proof that when it comes to rockin' out, nobody does it better.

But enough about AC/DC's regular record-breaking appearances at Donington. Let's roll the clock back again to 1981 and the birth of 'For Those About To Rock (We Salute You)'...

KERRANG!'S DONINGTON '91 SPECIAL

CHAPTER ELEVEN

CANNON FODDER

"Both rhythmically and lyrically, AC/DC were a groundbreaking band. Lyrically, they are up there with Bruce Springsteen, David Bowie and Ian Hunter in the way they portrayed a bright, colourful side of life. Rhythmically, nobody has come close to them in what they've done for rock 'n' roll. They are the equivalent of what Funk did for R'n'B. They're true innovators..."
– Nikki Sixx (Mötley Crüe)

A C/DC were officially credited as having recorded the greatest Metal song of all time, when 'Whole Lotta Rosie' was voted top Heavy Metal song in the very first issue of *Kerrang!*, published in June 1981. The poll had been conducted through the pages of *Sounds*, and 'Whole Lotta Rosie' wasn't the only entry from the band. Others were 'Let There Be Rock' (Number 18), 'Touch Too Much' (29), 'Highway To Hell' (39), 'Hell's Bells' (45), 'Walk Over You' (100), 'Back In Black' (104), 'Shot Down In Flames' (105) and 'Sin City' (107). What a compilation album *that* would make!

Not that Acca Dacca were spending an inordinate amount of time celebrating this huge success. They were far too busy in Paris working on the next album with 'Mutt' Lange. And hitting a few problems into the bargain. The main cause of concern was the fact that 'Mutt' was apparently finding it very difficult to get the right kind of sound for the record.

"We came to Paris ands went into Pathe-Marconi, which must be a good studio cos a lot of bands use it, but it just wasn't right for us," Brian told *Kerrang!*'s Steve Gett months later. "We went in thinking it was okay, but when we tried to get that LIVE sound we wanted on an

FOR THOSE ABOUT TO ROCK

album, it just didn't happen.

"And after a fortnight... 'Mutt' Lange said, 'This is hard work – we're missing the point'."

Thus, when the fivesome left France and headed to England to headline at Donington, things were up in the air. However, by the time the band returned hot-foot and triumphant from their feverish festival activities, Lange had solved the sound problems – by hiring a mobile studio from England – and recording ran smoothly.

The album, titled 'For Those About to Rock (We Salute You)', was released in November 1981, and quickly made an impact on the

UK charts, climbing to Number Three. So, what sort of album was this? This is how the band explained it, track-by-track, to *Kerrang!*'s Sylvie Simmons:

'For Those About To Rock (We Salute You)' – "We had this chorus riff and we thought, 'Well, this sounds rather deadly'. We were trying to find a good title, and there's this book from years ago about Roman gladiators called 'For Those About To Die We Salute You'. So we thought, 'for those about to rock'... I mean, it sounds better than 'for those about to die'," said Angus. "Actually, that song's got a lot of meaning to it. It's a very inspiring song. It makes you feel a bit powerful, and I think that's what rock 'n' roll is all about."

'Put The Finger On You' – "That's basically a gangster line, like they do in the movies," explained Angus. "We're not putting the finger on anyone in particular, it's always the other way round!"

'Let's Get It Up' – "Filth, pure filth. We're a filthy band," proclaimed Brian.

"It was just a line that sprang to mind," added Angus, "and it sounded better than, 'Let's Go Down'."

'Inject The Venom' – "That's a power thing," said Angus. "It's rather like 'For Those About To Rock...'. It means, 'Have it hot'."

"There's one line that says, *'If you inject the venom it will be your last attack'* – which is like a snake, once it bites you, it's got nothing left," concluded Brian.

'Snowballed' – "Meaning you've been conned, fooled again," explained Angus. "And

BACKSTAGE PASS FOR THE 'FOR THOSE ABOUT TO ROCK' TOUR

we figured we've been tricked enough in our time, so we came up with that. It could be the woman you're paying alimony to, anything."

'Evil Walks' – "As the name says, evil walks – it's everywhere!" proclaimed Angus. "When we were playing it at the beginning I said, 'Those chords sound dead evil'. And that's how we do it, just sitting around and nattering and jamming away. And someone says something like 'evil walks' and that's it."

'C.O.D.' – "Most people think of C.O.D. as 'Cash On Delivery', or 'Cash On Demand'. I was sitting around trying to come up with a better one, and I came up with 'Care Of The Devil'," opined Angus. "We're not black magic Satanists, or whatever you call it. I don't drink blood. I may wear black underwear now and then, but that's about it!"

'Breaking The Rules' – "It's like when someone says, 'You can't do that'. They were always saying that to me at school," admitted Angus. "You do it anyhow."

'Night Of The Long Knives' – "It sounded nice," was Angus' simple, straightforward description.

'Spellbound' – "That's a tricky one," shrugged Angus. "It's a slower one for us, but we liked it anyhow. It's one of those moody ones."

"You know when you get one of those days when it's like a trance," concluded Brian. "It's hard to describe really, but that's 'Spellbound'. We set it to a man driving a car, blinded by a bright beam. But it could be any situation."

There you have it – the Young/Johnson perspective at the time. But how did the critics react? Mark Putterford had this to say when he re-assessed the album for *Kerrang!* just prior to Donington '84: 'The once sleazy, dirty AC/DC were now a classy, highly tuned Rock machine. But the music didn't cruise on superstar pretensions as the band recorded their new album in Paris, once more with 'Mutt' Lange at the helm.

'Where once there was a one-and-a-half ton bell, there was now an arsenal of cannons, which saluted those of us about to rock. And plenty of us did to the slick 'n' shiny newies from Young, Young and Johnson like 'Put The Finger On You', 'Let's Get It Up', 'Evil Walks' and 'C.O.D..'

'However, For Those...' didn't quite match 'Back In Black' and several of the songs didn't work for me, as the band appeared to be searching for new ideas. 'Breaking The Rules' and 'Night Of The Long Knives' were below par, while 'Spellbound' was just rather tedious.'

Whatever the doubts in certain quarters about the merits or otherwise of 'For Those About To Rock...', it was a worldwide commercial success. And just prior to the LP's release, the band received a further boost when no less than seven of their albums appeared in *Kerrang!*'s All-Time Top 100 Heavy Metal Albums chart, compiled by votes cast by readers of the big *K!* and also *Sounds*. They were: 'If You Want Blood...' (Number Two, only kept out of the top slot by 'Rainbow Rising'), 'Back In Black' (Three), 'Highway To Hell' (Nine), 'Let There Be Rock' (40), 'Powerage' (51), 'High Voltage' (69) and 'Dirty Deeds Done Dirt Cheap' (82).

This was a sure sign of the band's enduring popularity among British Rock fans. In America, though, AC/DC were still increasing in fame. 'For Those About To Rock...' became their first chart-topping album on the other side of the Atlantic, and a huge tour of the States proved that they were attracting bigger audiences than ever.

Kerrang! despatched Sylvie Simmons to catch up with 'em during early 1982, when they played in Indianapolis. She was mightily impressed:

'Imaginary guitar heroes are standing on metal chairs, twitching. Imaginary guitar heroes who've had one too many quaaludes have fallen off chairs midway through a strenuous riff and are piled up twitching on the floor. The arena looks like it's filled with the kind of hopelessly diseased and uncontrollable bodies that benefit from a Jerry Lewis telethon. If they took their shirts off and lifted their trousers, they'd all look a lot like Angus Young.

'It wasn't such a good idea to spend half the day queuing outside in temperatures well below zero to get the best seats in the house. But that's what 17,000 rockers have just done with only alcohol to ward off frostbite. Inside, it smells like a distillery. Light a match and you'd put the majority of the young male population of 'The Crossroads Of America'... out of their misery.

'People are whooping at the big black curtains. From the blackness

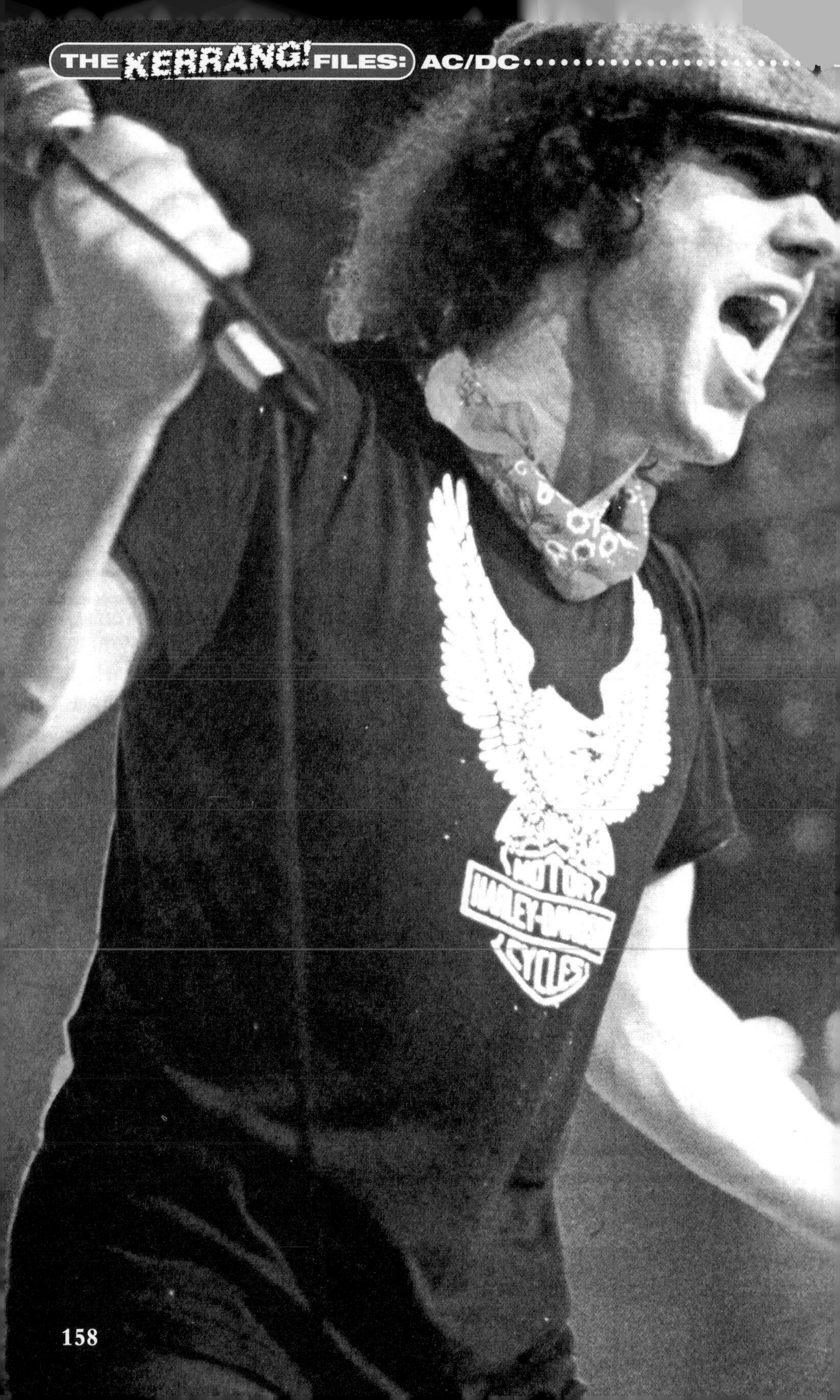
MOTOR
HARLEY-DAVIDSON
CYCLES

a bell starts tolling and the band goes on. All hell breaks loose. "Whooaaaargh!!" screams Brian Johnson, stomping the stage like a working-class rhino, all flat cap and beer belly, charged and horny. "Whooaaaargh!!" echoes Indianapolis, as people drop their bottles and their banners and their girlfriends to get down to the serious business of imaginary soloing and air-punching. 'Hell's Bells' starts off an hour-and-a-half of hot and heavy bludgeoning Rock...

' 'Sin City', 'Back In Black', 'The Jack', 'Highway To Hell', 'Dirty Deeds', 'Whole Lotta Rosie', 'Let There Be Rock'... with a couple of exceptions it's your basic best of AC/DC set, the only difference from last year's best of AC/DC set being the cannons during the encore, exploding with smoke in time to the newest AC/DC anthem, 'For Those About To Rock...'.'

'AC/DC are still the best Hard Rock band in the world. Angus, nutty Angus, head down, rocketing across the stage, falling to his knees, shaking sweat over the madmen in the first 10 rows, mounting the speakers, lying on his back, kicking the air like

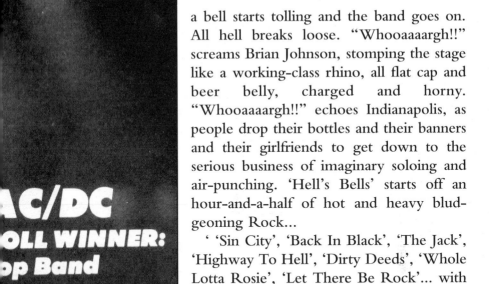

AC/DC
POLL WINNER:
Top Band

POLL WINNERS

BAND

1. AC/DC
2. RUSH
3. MOTORHEAD
4. Whitesnake
5. Gillan
6. Saxon
7. Status Quo
8. Black Sabbath
9. Rainbow
10. Kiss

MALE SINGER

AC/DC TOP THE FIRST *KERRANG!* READERS' POLL

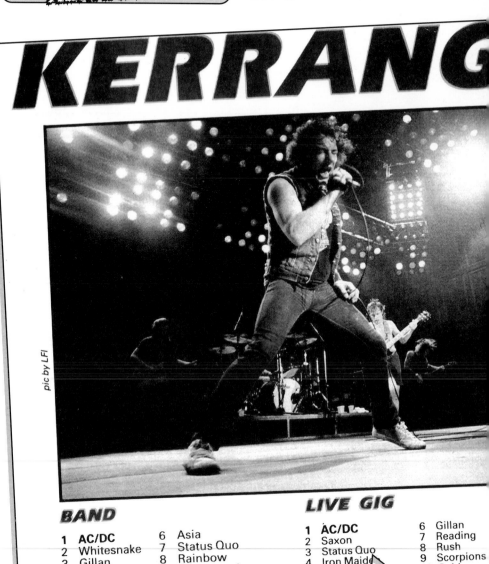

KERRANG

pic by LFI

BAND

1 AC/DC
2 Whitesnake
3 Gillan
4 Iron Maiden
5 R..h

6 Asia
7 Status Quo
8 Rainbow
9 Motorhead
.. Scorpion

LIVE GIG

1 AC/DC
2 Saxon
3 Status Quo
4 Iron Maide..
5 Diamond ..ead

6 Gillan
7 Reading
8 Rush
9 Scorpions
10 Spider

AC/DC SCOOP THE *KERRANG!* READERS' POLL FOR THE SECOND YEAR RUNNING, REFLECTING THEIR SUCCESS IN 1982

some American brat who wasn't given his Breakfast Of Champions with the free plastic battleship. Jumping onto Johnson's shoulders, taking his tamed cordless guitar on walkies through the audience on the back of a bouncer... Then standing in the centre of a stream of lights, an unlikely but brilliant guitar hero, while the crowd raves on

982

GUITAR

1 **ANGUS YOUNG**
2 Ritchie Blackmore
3 Michael Schenker
4 Dave Muray
5 Alex Lifeson
6 Steve Howe
7 Gary Moore
8 Randy Rhoads
9 Eddie Van Halen
10 Jimmy Page

BASS

1 **CLIFF WILLIAMS**
2 Geddy Lee
3 Steve Harris
4 John Wetton
5 John McCoy
6 Geezer Butler
7 Neil Murray
8 Lemmy
9 Roger Glover
10 Gene Simmons

DRUMS

at the Thunder from Down Under. By the third encore the cannons fire and the amps are screaming. So's the audience. So are my ears as I head backstage, but there's still a smile on my face.'

Get the picture? The band were now HUGE news in the States.

Backstage, Brian Johnson was in fine fettle, if suffering just a tad from having played a game of racquetball.

"I thought it was me f★★king appendix about to blow up," he told Sylvie. "But it's just a f★★king stitch. I played racquetball for the first time. It's just like squash – and I f★★king ran into the wall. We're all hitting each other with racquets, because we didn't know what the f★★k we were doing. And I thought I was fit! It killed us."

On this US tour, the band were beginning to attract a higher percentage of females, both out front and backstage. But Johnson, for one, wasn't in the least bit interested in partaking of the pleasures of the flesh.

"You never f★★k them! You leave them alone. There's nasty diseases going around America, I'll tell you! You shake hands and that's it. That's for the crew – they're the ones with backstage passes, not us! We have good, clean fun, y'know – a quick game of cards and all that. I'm saying nothing. Me, I'm married with two kids...

"Thing is, though, these gigs in America – the boys were sitting 'round in the dressing room last week and saying that this is the first time they've actually heard girls scream at them? Because in England, it's nearly all lads. Most of the audience is fellas in America as well,

161

but since we started this tour there's been a lot of girls. I don't know: I think it's because we're on the f★★king radio so much. I don't think it can be me good looks...

"Funny thing is, we've been going great on this tour. All the gigs have sold out, real big places too. Last time we played Indianapolis, we played to about 4,000. Tonight, what is there? 17,000? And it's brand new audiences... But it's funny here tonight, playing songs like 'Sin City', because it shows in their faces that they don't know what the f★★k it is! The only albums they've bought so far are 'Highway To Hell', 'Back In Black' and 'Dirty Deeds Done Dirt Cheap'."

But all this attention did have its 'down' side. Because of their popularity, AC/DC were the favoured target at the time for Bible-thumpers, who saw them as some form of Satanic influence on the fans. Angus was suitably unimpressed:

"They've been bothering us for some years. Some crud sent me a letter, addressed to Bon too, sending us these stupid things. Some people are sick! If they want to go God-bothering, they should go God-bother the Pope. He needs it. We don't."

Back in Britain, the band's absence throughout much of 1982 had no negative effect whatsoever on their following. Indeed, 'Let's Get It Up' reached Number 13 in the charts during February, followed a few months later by a Number 15 placement for the title cut from the album.

Finally, the 'Cannon And Bell' tour (as this trek had been dubbed) reached the UK during late September. And this time, the band moved out of the halls and into the arenas, playing the likes of the Birmingham NEC and Wembley Arena in London. *Kerrang!* announced the full list of dates in early July, proclaiming the band as 'possibly the biggest grossing Rock band in the world'. The dates were Birmingham NEC September 29/30, Manchester Apollo October 3, Newcastle City Hall 4-6, Glasgow Apollo 8/9, Edinburgh Playhouse 10/11, London Wembley Arena 18/19.

Geoff Banks was suitably impressed when he reviewed one of the shows in Newcastle for *Kerrang!*:

'After a none too impressive Reading (Festival) appearance, Y&T (the support band on this tour) have obviously got their act together and seem more at home than in front of a non-committed crowd, and seize on the opportunity let fly on all cylinders...

'Now to the main reason for my jaunt to the netherlands of Newcastle – to see the *numero uno* Rock band on our planet at this moment in time. The crowd are packed in like sardines a good half-hour before the show starts, with the most ardent poised in the aisles ready to rush the security stockade the second anything starts to happen onstage.

'With the dimming of the lights, a buzz of anticipation spreads through the gathered multitude and, on cue, the haunting toll of the bell signals the arrival of the band. The curtains peel back and without further ado they surge into 'Hell's Bells'. Bathed in red, blue and green light, Angus is sombrely poised centre stage, while the rest of the band kick out that familiar rhythm behind Brian's barbed wire vocals.

'As ever, the emphasis is on that good old sexual beat topped with lashings of stunning guitar work. Yet Angus is only one side of the coin. If asked to define the real driving force behind AC/DC, I would have to say Malcolm's relentless chugging riffs that, combined with Phil and Cliff's metronome bass end punching, make for a rhythm that you could set a watch by.

' 'Shot Down In Flames' sustains the excitement and goes a long way towards proving that 'For Those About To Rock...' is not within spitting distance of the old material, as is made clear by the frenzied state of the crowd and echoed by the effort of the band – though Angus drips sweat on every number while at the same time duck-walking his way into the R'n'R history books...

'Despite having played (these) songs hundreds of times before, they still manage to inject vitality into them in a way that most ever-trucking bands fail to achieve, and after running through all the old faves, including an anthemic version of 'Whole Lotta Rosie', they leave the stage to...a roar...'

By the end of 1982, AC/DC's position as the top Rock band around was cemented when *Kerrang!* published the results of its readers' poll. The boys were voted 'Top Band', Angus was 'Top Guitarist', Cliff was 'Top Bassist', the band were voted as having produced the 'Best Live Gig', and 'For Those About To Rock...' was the 'Best Single'. In addition, Johnson was third top male vocalist (behind Ian

■*Backstage at one of their recent Hammersmith Odeon shows, **AC/DC** were presented with a gold disc for their '**For Those About To Rock**' album. Our picture shows Angus and co in the delightful company of two schoolgirls (well, Atlantic Records' **Mary Hooton** and **Jayne Haynes**, actually!)...*

AC/DC ARE PRESENTED WITH A GOLD DISC FOR 'FOR THOSE ABOUT TO ROCK', 1982

Gillan and David Coverdale), Phil Rudd was second best drummer (behind Cozy Powell), 'Let's Get It Up' finished sixth best single, and Angus was amazingly second (to David Coverdale) as 'Male Pin-Up'. Only Malcolm failed to score in the poll.

When told about their huge success in the poll 'Jonna' reacted to Kerrang!'s Steve Gett: "I'm chuffed to bits. I've just been talking to the lads (the band were then in Paris), and they're chuffed as well. It's weird because we've been so quiet this year, not having an album to push, so it's a real good boost...

"We released 'For Those About To Rock...' just before Christmas 1981, and never actually did anything until a couple of months ago. But the British gigs were great and we were knocked out by the audiences. Now, we've come out to Europe and we still haven't got anything to push, and it's pretty hard. We've been grafting our bollocks off, but we've had some great shows. And it's nice to know that the kids keep turning up to see us."

As for future plans, Johnson stated: "We're grafting on one now. I love albums, but again you've gotta think of the lads. They've been doing albums year after year for eight years now. We should start recording about February, though."

Johnson also took time out to express his disappointment at the way in which Geordie product was being released to capitalise on his high profile with Acca Dacca.

"I'm pissed off for the other lads in Geordie because I don't think they're receiving a penny in royalties. I'm fighting a case against it at the moment, but I don't know what'll happen. It's just getting beyond a joke. It's a rip-off – a pain in the arse."

So 1983 dawned, with the band for once on an extended break. Nothing was planned for the first half of the year. But there were rumblings in the distance...

CHAPTER TWELVE

SWITCHED ON, FIRED UP!

"AC/DC are some of my closest friends in the music business. I've known them all for years, and they're among the most down-to-earth and easy-going people you could wish to meet..."
– Ronnie James Dio (Dio)

Eschewing their by-now traditional trip to the studios as a new year dawned, AC/DC elected instead to take an extended break – a chance for limbs, spirit and hearts to recover after the enormous stresses and strains of a huge world tour under the most intense of scrutiny. No longer a happy-go-lucky bunch playing down the road to a handful of fans, Acca Dacca were a huge concern, generating millions of pounds for record label, management and a whole host of other employees, as well as themselves.

At the start of '83, Malcolm Young and Phil Rudd headed back to Australia to relax and prepare for the next round of activity, whilst Cliff Williams took off to Hawaii with his wife Georgeann – for a chance to spend some time at a recently-purchased house – and Angus jetted to Holland. Brian Johnson, meantime, was finally forced for tax reasons to leave his beloved Newcastle, and elected to set up home in Florida.

What this break did for the band was allow them a chance to con-

AC/DC 1983
(FROM LEFT):
BRIAN JOHNSON,
ANGUS YOUNG,
SIMON WRIGHT,
MALCOLM YOUNG,
CLIFF WILLIAMS

sider their position – and, more importantly, the positions of those around them. This led to changes. Out went manager Peter Mensch and the CCC organisation, with tour manager Ian Jeffreys basically asked to take over the day-to-day running of the band overseen by Malcolm, who had now emerged as the business brain and powerbroker within AC/DC.

Also not retained was 'Mutt' Lange. Acca Dacca now decided that, whilst they would return to Compass Point Studios to record the new album, Lange's smooth approach to production wasn't in their best interests. They wanted to spice things up and generate a much more dynamic, live sound. To this end, Tony Platt (who hadn't been involved with 'For Those ABout To Rock' because of prior commitments) was brought back in an engineering capacity, with the band producing themselves.

There was a tense atmosphere surrounding the band at the time. They were pulling in their horns, tightening up the organisation in order to keep outsiders just that – outside. There was a sense of mistrust within the band, fuelled to some extent by the stress of keeping this mega-outfit on the rails. Perhaps the pressure of coping with Bon's death was also finally taking its toll. They'd hardly had a break since that fateful day. Now, tensions were bubbling to the surface. According to insiders, the atmosphere at Compass Point was far from jocular.

One amusing story did emerge at the time, alleging that although Lange wasn't directly involved with the new album, tapes of the recordings were being flown back to England for him to make comments and suggestions. This story first appeared in an American publication, and was then reported in *Kerrang!*. Unfortunately, it wasn't true! Well, we all make mistakes.

As recording got into its stride, Phil Rudd was fired. Word reached *Kerrang!* during early June that the drummer had departed. But at the time, no reasons were given for his sudden disappearance from the camp, nor on who would be drafted in.

It was only some time later that the real reason emerged for Rudd's dismissal: the sticksman himself admitted to having indulged too much in the high life. Things got so bad that on the last part of the 'Cannon And Bell' tour, he was hallucinating about finding strangers in his room. The break back home in Australia seemed to allow Rudd to get his act together. But having raced through his drum parts for the new album, he was left with precious little to do in Nassau – and the old problems re-emerged.

To make matters worse, there were personal difficulties between Malcolm and Phil. Their relationship progressively deteriorated, to the point where a physical confrontation eventually took place. That was the last straw. Two hours later, Rudd was flying home. He was out, electing to retire to New Zealand where he bought a helicopter business and gave up professional music completely. Fortunately, he managed to iron out most of his problems, and he does re-enter the AC/DC story later on in this book.

Meantime, though, the band finished off the new record (to be titled 'Flick Of The Switch'), and the rumours started circulated in the media as to who would replace Rudd. *Kerrang!* threw the name of former Roxy Music and Angelic Upstarts skinsman Paul Thompson into the fray as an opening salvo. But this took a temporary back seat as the new album's release approached. Originally, it was to be titled 'I Want To Rock', and *Kerrang!* duly announced this fact during early August, only for the final title to be confirmed two weeks later.

'The album (set for a late August release) has been produced by the band themselves,' quoth *Kerrang!* as full details of the album came to the fore. 'According to personages who've copped an earful of the platter, it has a rather primitive feel reminiscent of the Aussies' formative days.'

'Flick Of The Switch' saw the light of day in time for a review to appear in the landmark 50th issue of the Big *K!* from the author:

'When you've clambered to the top of the rocky mountain, there are two options open. You can either enjoy the brief taste of rarified fortunes, breathe in deeply and dare anyone to knock you off. Or else you can look down and realise just how far you can fall.

'Superficially at least, AC/DC could be accused of taking the second path. For having reached for the twinkling stars via the phenomenal 'Back In Black', they wobbled somewhat with 'For Those About To Rock...' and have seemingly gone for 'desperation measures' this time around: parting company with producer 'Mutt' Lange to do all that side of affairs themselves, plus returning to a basic approach.

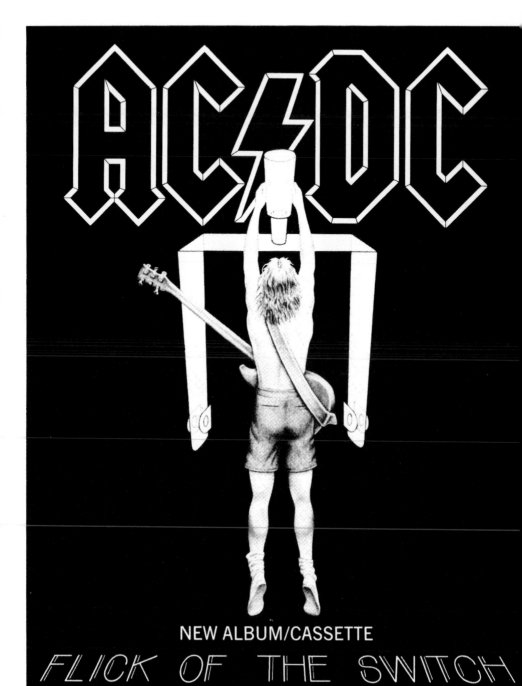

'So, is this the last-gasp of a dying giant? Wrong, buster! True, 'Flick...' is not as satisfyingly remarkable as was 'Back In Black'. However, it is a considerable improvement on 'For Those...'. Yes, the band have returned to their early rock 'n' roll style, but they've taken with them the vital lessons of pacing, dynamism and craftsmanship learnt over the past several years.

'Thus, whilst everything is kept simple, more direct and snappy (no hint of over-cluttered Lange overkill here), nonetheless the album lacks nothing in tightness and rounded atmospherics. And the band actually come across as lean 'n' hungry once again. Obviously, the two-year gap between 'For Those...' and this 'ere *oeuvre* hasn't done 'em any harm. Brian Johnson bursts forth with some voraciously rasping throatmanship, whilst Angus' unmistakable lead breaks (all belching Boogie and knife-sharp thrusts) as usual give everything that extra dimension.

'Let's not forget, either, the superb rhythm section of Malcolm Young, Cliff Williams and Phil Rudd (how AC/DC are gonna miss their Rudd-er behind the kit!). As solid as hardened cement (tough on outside and tough on the inside), once again these three prove themselves the very best 'beat meat' machine in HM.

'But what about the material? Overall, it's consistently good, never falling to any unacceptable level – mediocrity thankfully is one word that won't have to be evoked as an apt description of anything here.

'The style is very much in the same vogue as that adopted on the last two platters. A mid-tempo diet, with most songs building steadily from a deliberately controlled platform and culminating in a punchy chorus. Nothing here sticks out as an orthodox Pop song, yet everything has the standard Pop number structure. What AC/DC have become adept at is manipulating the basic 'mainstream music' formula so that maximum impact and power is obtained from their own numbers with minimal reliance on old-hat tricks like ultra-speed and grotesque soloing.

'Of course, die-hard Metallica disciples will find most cuts here pedestrian. But they're essentially missing the point. When

ADVERT FOR THE 'FLICK OF THE SWITCH' LP, 1983

approached in the right manner, controlled aggression can be infinite-ly more lethal than a rock 'n' roll blur. Besides, having the vast major-ity of tracks set up in the 'trotting' vein means that when the band enter into a full gallop (as on the title number, 'Landslide', which is disconcertingly like a Rose Tattoo outtake, and 'Brain Shaker'), the impact is that much greater.

'And amongst the uniformly impressive ditties lie two absolute gems, viz 'Nervous Shakedown' and 'Badlands'. It's not so much that this pair are radically different from anything else here (although the latter does contain some nifty bottleneck guitar work from Angus) which make 'em outstanding. No, it's more a case of everything gelling to perfection. So there you have it, two masterpieces and eight other good-to-strong numbers. I'd say that constitutes good value for money, wouldn't you?'

"The album is a really good Rock album, that's all it is," 'Jonna' told *Kerrang!*'s Chris Watts. "We weren't trying to do anything else, we just wanted another album that would burn! It's a little different this time, because we didn't have a producer, which turned out to be an advantage. Like, we had our own thoughts and there was no out-side influence to stop us. It was a struggle at times to produce our-selves, but that was half the fun of it. We found ourselves getting trapped by producers who wanted something different from us, so this time we thought, 'Bollocks to 'em. We'll do it ourselves!'...

"It's also nice now to be in a position where we can put something back – like, I've just opened this studio up in Newcastle for young bands who want to have a go at it. There are many people out there, really talented people, who just don't get the breaks that we did, and so I'd like to do me bit to lend them a hand."

At this stage in the proceedings, the band also announced the name of their new drummer. He was 20-year-old Simon Wright, who had previously worked with virtual unknowns Tora! Tora!, AIIZ and Tytan.

Originally from the Manchester area, Wright had recorded one single with Tora! Tora! (namely 'Red Sun Setting'), before joining

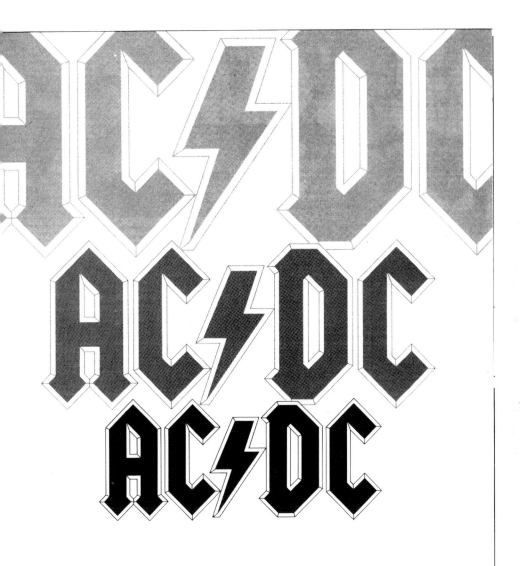

NEW SINGLE
GUNS FOR HIRE
A 9774

THE KERRANG! FILES: AC/DC ················

SINGLES

reviewed by Steve Joule

Songs that would have had Gloria Swanson eat her piles out.

KISS: 'Lick It Up' (Casablanca)

I can just picture Eddie Yeats giving Marion one round the back of his dustcart whilst this little ditty comes gently wafting out of the cab window. Music for making rock 'n' roll babies to. A damn fine record of the highest quality, the sort of stuff you've heard a thousand times before but oh! Lordy never quite as well done as it is on this piece of plastic. CLASSIC ROCK 'N' ROLL.

AC/DC: 'Guns For Hire' (Atlantic)

This one has certainly been giving the neighbours heart-failure over the last few weeks. Never mind, all that exercise banging on the wall has probably done them the world of good. Again it's the sort of stuff you've heard many times before but some people just seem to be able to knock it out and make it sound as fresh as a daisy. A wall-shaker of the finest calibre – thank the Gods mine are made from reinforced concrete.

WAYSTED: 'Women In Chains' (Chrysalis)

***KERRANG!* REVIEWS 'GUNS FOR HIRE', 1983**

AIIZ and recording the live 'Witch Of Berkeley' LP for Polydor in 1980. However, that particular act fell apart, going on to release just one more record (a single titled 'I'm The One Who Loves You') prior to splitting up. By late 1982, Wright, having relocated to London, was recruited to join the so-called NWOBHM 'supergroup' Tytan. Wright was drafted in to replace former Judas Priest man Les Binks as the band worked on their debut album (tentatively titled 'Rough Justice') for Kamikaze Records. However, financial problems eventually buried Tytan, leaving an unfinished album and Wright kicking his heels in frustration.

After spasmodic gigging, Tytan called it a day in the Summer of 1983. It was then that the following ad appearing in the music press:

'Heavy Rock drummer wanted. If you don't hit hard, don't apply'.

This was AC/DC's third attempt at finding the right man to take over from Rudd. Whilst still recording at Compass Point, they'd flown in a selection of drummers, all to no avail. Later on, when the album was being mixed in New York, another batch were tried out – again with no success.

The band returned to London facing a hectic touring schedule, but with no replacement in sight. So they took the decision to place an ad in the British music press. They didn't put their name into the advert to discourage time-wasters. They then hired Nomis rehearsal studios in West London to hold the auditions.

In order to filter out those simply not good enough, the band had a separate room through which all candidates were ushered. In there was a roadie, a drum kit and a tape machine. Only if the drummer was good enough to play along to a tape of the band and impress the waiting roadie would they be allowed into the room where AC/DC themselves were waiting. Through this process came Simon Wright.

"I was shocked, to tell you the truth," Wright admitted to Chris Watts, about how he felt upon finding out who the band behind the advert were. "I didn't know who the band were, and when I went down to rehearsals I was a bit taken aback. But the lads made me feel comfortable and auditioning was a doddle for me, because I've loved the band for a long time. The main appeal for me is simply that Malcolm and Angus write brilliant songs. I remember Malcolm just telling me to treat the whole thing as if it were a club band, and it is that sort of atmosphere. There are no egos pulling in different directions."

Strangely enough, it was only when the band invited Wright to sit down with 'em whilst they discussed touring arrangements that he realised he was probably in AC/DC! By October, the young Mancunian had made his live debut in Vancouver, Canada. And just a few dates later, Wright found himself indirectly embroiled in trouble, when the Tacoma Dome in Seattle was nearly set alight when a fan fired a rocket into the ceiling, which exploded with potentially fatal consequences. Fortunately a tragedy was averted. And which song were the band playing when all of this happened? 'This House Is On Fire'!

IT'S THE time of year when all good schoolboys go back to work. And, naturally enough, good ole Angus Young and his troops have begun a fresh term. The latest Aussie LP, 'Flick Of The Switch', (their ninth for Atlantic) is the first one to be *totally* produced by the band alone and seems likely to add a few units to their overall sales figure (worldwide) of virtually 25 million copies shifted from 'High Voltage' to 'For Those About To Rock'. In addition, expect a single from the lads in late September/early October, although at present no decision has been made as to which track will be chosen.

The band, in fact, will soon be starting a massive US tour, which will take them through – with scarcely a break in the itinerary – until Christmas. And this will mark the debut with AC/DC for new drummer Simon Wright (who replaces Phil Rudd). Aged 20, Wright was formerly with Mancunian band AIIZ (appearing on their one-and-only *Polydor* LP, 'Witch Of Berkeley'), and Tytan.

However, UK fans of the band will have to wait some time before they can judge for themselves how Wright is shaping up, as AC/DC have no plans to tour here this year.   MALCOLM DOME

ANGUS YOUNG

But what of British dates? Back in December, 'Jonna' had told Chris Watts of *Kerrang!*: "Well, we're going to finish up here (the US) first, and then basically play it all by ear, because I hate planning my life, you know? We'll have a talk when we finish and no doubt Europe – that includes you lot – will come up somewhere. We'll have about a week off, which will be enjoyable and then we'll decide what to do. We'll probably just get off the plane at Gatwick or something, and suddenly decide there and then that we're going to start a tour in four minutes!"

The truth was a little less spontaneous, as UK audiences had to make do with just one date on the 'Flick Of The Switch' tour – at Donington in August 1984. This lack of profile was reflected in the results of the 1984 *Kerrang!* readers' poll. AC/DC won no category whatsoever, ending up as fifth top band, with ninth best single ('Nervous Shakedown'). 'Jonna' was ninth top vocalist, Angus was fourth best guitarist and Donington was third top gig. But the band were also granted the 'accolade' of being considered eighth biggest bore/disappointment of the year.

The fab five finally brought the whole 18-month shebang to a climactic conclusion at the first ever Rock In Rio festival from January 11-20, 1985. *Kerrang!* despatched writer Mick Wall and photographer Ross Halfin to cover this event. The pair found themselves seated close to AC/DC on the flight out to this spectacular event.

'Over the years,' wrote Wall, 'AC/DC have acquired the unhappy habit of completely ignoring the existence of any living thing outside their own familiar sphere. Very little of any cogent value lies outside their own sightless cosmology of band managers, roadies, bodyguards and immediate family members. Malcolm Young nods a 'hi' to Ross, and Ross offers a copy of the new *Kerrang!* to drummer Simon Wright. Simon sneers into Ross' face and declines. Us and AC/DC, we don't get on any more...'

Not an auspicious start for the *K!* duo. However, that was a minor irritation. This was, after all, an occasion so special and impressive that such incidents were irrelevant. Rock In Rio was designed to open up

THE AUTHOR REVEALS AC/DC'S TOURING PLANS IN *KERRANG!*, 1983

Brazil to contemporary music, especially Rock music. There was a huge market out there waiting to be tapped. The likes of Queen, Rod Stewart, Ozzy Osbourne, Whitesnake, Iron Maiden, Yes, the Scorpions and AC/DC were persuaded to spend some time in the Brazilian sun.

Whilst everyone seemed to have a good time and parties were apparently held on every corner in Rio, AC/DC kept their now traditional low profile.

For the record, Acca Dacca did two slots at the festival. Both were well received by the fanatical crowds. For Wright, though, it was a strange experience.

"It was odd being in the Third World with all that poverty. It was real sad, seeing all those shanty towns and beggars and kids with nothing on their feet, just yards from big flash hotels and tourists loaded with money," he would recall a few years on.

On the first night they performed, Great Train Robber Ronnie Biggs turned up on the side of the stage! And the band were being constantly assailed by the smell of hamburgers wafting from a huge McDonald's stand set up in the middle of the site!

Rock In Rio (which was supposed to become an annual event) was something of a disaster. The site, specially built for the occasion at a cost of more than $11 million was eventually destroyed and a huge amount of money was lost. Still, to be asked to play at such a global event was an honour; further proof of the band's major status – not that any were needed.

After Rio? Rest – and lots of it. AC/DC took another lengthy break, in order to gird their loins for action during the Spring of 1985...

KERRANG! TALKS EXCLUSIVELY TO BRIAN JOHNSON IN 1983

IF THE CAP FITS. . .

x by Chris Walter

BRIAN JOHNSON *wears it we sez Chris*

CHAPTER THIRTEEN

FLYING IN OVERDRIVE

"I like rhythm 'n' blues, I like rock 'n' roll. AC/DC I like a lot: very loud!"
– Stephen King (top Horror author)

"**W**e felt it might be becoming a bit predictable, going around the same places every year – people might get the attitude of, 'Ah, we won't bother seeing them this year, they'll be back again next year!'. It's a bit like a circus coming to town, you know. And there was 10 years of doing that, so I think it's quite understandable to take a break."

That was the way Malcolm Young explained the fact that the band elected to take time off after the Rock In Rio experience, before getting stuck into recording the next album.

It wasn't until the Spring of '85 that AC/DC regrouped to work on what was to become the 'Fly On The Wall' album. They holed up in Mountain Studios out in Montreux, Switzerland, which was a former casino. Again, the band produced themselves; in particular, Angus and Malcolm took control of this side of things, and the recording process flowed smoothly enough, with the band once more going for a raw, live feel – something they felt showcased their talents to best effect. This time around, they brought in engineer Mark Dearnley to get the requisite sounds.

During early April, there were reports that Brian Johnson had quit the band and gone back home to Newcastle. This stemmed from a

183

**THE 'FLY ON THE WALL'
SLEEVE, 1985**

comment made by a major American manager which subsequently got blown out of all proportion by *Kerrang!* snapper Ross Halfin. He told the *K!* editorial staff that Johnson had definitely quit the band.

However, assiduous research proved that this wasn't at all true. Indeed, 'Jonna' was working hard on the AC/DC album. In an act of 'retribution' on the hapless photographer, *Kerrang!* convinced him that AC/DC had indeed parted company with Johnson – and that David Coverdale was the new singer! Halfin fell for this wind-up to the extent that a couple of weeks later he actually bumped into the Whitesnake mainman – and refused to believe his protestations that he hadn't joined Acca Dacca!

What *was* true was that Jonna had signed a solo deal with Red Bus Records and was planning a solo project when time allowed.

On June 28, the band finally unleashed the new album. How was it received? *Kerrang!*'s Mark Putterford had this to say on reflection: 'The finished album wasn't one of AC/DC's best, and even their staunchest fans had to admit it. Side One proved to be far stronger than the flip, but in essence 'Fly On The Wall' lacked the style of 'Back In Black', the songs of 'For Those About To Rock...' and the edge of 'Flick Of The Switch'.

'Its highlights were, without question, the title track, 'Shake Your Foundations' and, perhaps best of all, 'Sink The Pink'... When the band got the balance of groove, melody and energy just right they were still capable of mixing it with the best, but most of the rest of the album sounded lacklustre. 'Danger' (which was the first single lifted from this opus) plodded rather laboriously. 'Stand Up' was instantly forgettable... In fact, half of the songs on 'Fly On The Wall' wouldn't have made it onto any post-'Let There Be Rock' AC/DC album.'

However, despite the general critical thumbs-down, the album did reach Number Seven in the UK charts. And Malcolm Young rigorously defended the record in *Kerrang!*: "We spent a year on this album – about a year on writing songs and pre-production. We thought we'd sit back a bit this time. There was no pressure on us for another album or anything, so we thought we'd take a bit more time, and I think it's come out better as a result.

"We've got a set style, and when you've done so many albums and you've got to come up with something without repeating yourself, get songs that are good and don't require too much overdubbing... in some ways it's much harder to be simple than be involved."

In addition to the album, there was also a 28-minute long-form video titled 'Fly On The Wall', featuring a quintet of songs from the album performed live by the band in a New York club against a backdrop of some very dodgy-looking characters, seen from the viewpoint of a cartoon fly (the same one used on the album cover). The whole thing, directed by Brian Ward, was a little silly but had a certain sense of fun.

The band began their lengthy 'Fly...' world tour with another visit

185

to the States. However, towards the end of the year they announced five UK shows for January 1986 in *Kerrang!*: Whitley Bay Ice Rink 14, London Wembley Arena 16, Birmingham NEC 20, Edinburgh Playhouse 22 and 23. A couple of weeks later, the band announced a further date, at Manchester Apollo on January 13.

Back in the States, things were not going without a hitch. In fact, there was one rather major hitch. He was called Richard Ramirez, a 25-year-old Texan 'drifter' who brought AC/DC's name into disrepute, as reported by *Kerrang!*: 'Ramirez is a gruesome guy who performed Satanic rituals inspired by AC/DC songs, murdered 16 people and reportedly committed dozens of rapes.

'The lunatic Ramirez, who was finally arrested in LA, claims that AC/DC's initials stand for 'Anti-Christ/Devil's Child'. His deadly lurking activities were allegedly inspired by the song 'Night Prowler', on the band's 'Highway To Hell' album.'

When finally arrested, Ramirez was wearing an AC/DC T-shirt. He'd even left hats emblazoned with the band's logo at the scene of a number of his crimes.

"We've had a lot of shit thrown at us in the States – and that episode with the 'Night Stalker' (as Ramirez became known) didn't help," Malcolm Young told Mark Putterford of *Kerrang!* early in 1986. "Some kid was done for murder a couple of months ago and there was a mass of publicity about it. Now, this kid had an AC/DC T-shirt on – which immediately put the focus on us – and, of course, the religious fanatics – who've always followed us around over here – put 'Night Stalker' and 'Night Prowler' together. What they can't see is that 'Night Prowler' is just about creeping in at night on a couple of old girlfriends and doing the business – having a bit of fun, y'know? It's not about raping and pillaging...

"That whole thing with the 'Night Stalker' came about because he had an AC/DC T-shirt on when they pulled him in, and one of his friends said he was AC/DC mad. So what? Some loopy loves your band and wears your T-shirt while he's bumping off people – we're not telling the guy to do it!"

ANGUS YOUNG ON THE 'WHO MADE WHO' VIDEO SET, 1986

The fall-out from the Ramirez affair affected the US tour in certain areas, where the religious zealots who had dogged the band ever since they first went to America saw their chance to do some serious damage, as Malcolm explained to Putterford:

"We were due to play at the Springfield Auditorium in Illinois, when we heard that these religious fanatics had managed to get us banned by complaining that we were Satanists or whatever. So we spoke to a few people about it and found that these loonies were not allowed to do this kind of thing, and we could take them to court about it. So that's exactly what we did, and we won.

"The only thing was that the people who run the hotels in the area refused to let us stay in any of the local hotels, so we ended up having to spend the night before about 100 miles away and drive into town on the night of the show."

However, for the most part, the band's US tour went well. And at the start of 1986, they brought in new management.

"Now we're back on the road again, we need someone to handle the affairs offstage, to take some of the load off us – and that's why we've brought in Part Rock (also responsible for Gary Moore)," Malcolm told Mark Putterford. And as far as touring was concerned, even after all these years, Malcolm for one was all fired up:

"It is hard sometimes, but the minute you walk onstage and you hear the kids cheering and you see all the smiling faces, the hairs on the back of your neck stand up, and all of a sudden you're alive and ready to rock 'n' roll all night. Having Brian in the band keeps us all amused! He's a real joker – he's always laughing and fooling around – so how can we get fed up with him around?"

As far as the band's stage set was concerned...

"There's no new gimmicks or anything this time – we still use the cannon and the bell because they go over so well with the kids. Tracks like 'For Those About To Rock...' are such favourites that they'll probably always be with the band. If we dropped them, the kids would wanna know why!

"But with those kinda songs, we like to keep them until the end – when we've already finished our set – so that we don't think the gimmicks have got us the encores, y'know? That's what I like about them things – we've earned our encore through our songs, and then we come on and go BANG! with our gimmicks to kinda finish it all off nicely."

What exactly did the kids get this time for their money? Over to Sylvie Simmons, *K!*'s woman on the spot at Wembley Arena:

'Stomping and cavorting. Stomp. Stomp. From the minute I said goodbye to something long and wet and a-pound-a-glass in the bar and took to my metal seat, the big fat sleazy no-good-stomp-of-a-beat squatted in my braincell where it sits to this day. By the end of the show, it'd applied for a permanent residence, leaving me in a happy haze of battled boogiewoogiedom. And if you want a translation, it was GOOD.

'An AC/DC gig is a night on the skids with an old, old pal. Ain't likely to do much different after all these years, but you know you're gonna stagger home deaf, dumb and arseholed with a smile on your face and a beat in your braincell. They yell at us. We roar at them. And the Wembley speakers explode with one big, boozy, air-punching stomper after the next. 'Back In Black', second song in, one of the finest songs that ever drew blood. 'You Shook Me All Night Long', one of the finest etc., just a couple later, as stomping, filthy and stirring as a song can get. 'Sin City' (introduced as the perfect song for London...).

'Oh yeah, new stuff too, great greasy dollops of it, with 'Shake Your Foundations' coming out tops on the HM anthem scale. And two great golden cannons for those about to be deafened as the grander-than-grand finale... Sure, AC/DC are always the same. But the good thing about always doing it the same is that after all this time, they've got it right. Hell, they've got it right!'

In short, the show (which also saw Fastway as the support act) wasn't bad!

After the UK, the band spent a brief period in Europe, returning to the UK during mid-February to work on the video for a new song titled 'Who Made Who', which had been recorded with the original production team of Vanda and Young at Compass Point just after the US tour had been completed. So what was all this in aid of?

Whilst touring America, the band had been approached by top Horror author and major AC/DC fan Stephen King to ask permission to use some old material for the soundtrack of a forthcoming movie titled 'Maximum Overdrive' that he had written and on which he was to make his directorial debut. This idea then mushroomed when King suggested the band should record some new material for it. Thus, a reunion with Vanda and Young was effected.

"I always think that we did the great Rock tunes when we worked with my brother," said Angus to *Kerrang!*'s Dante Bonutto. "I like what we did with him better than the stuff we did with 'Mutt' Lange. 'Mutt' was very conscious of what was popular in America, but with my brother... if it was a rock 'n' roll song, he made sure it rocked!"

Whilst out in Compass Point, the band also recorded two instrumentals for the movie, namely 'D.T.' and 'Chase The Ace'. And King actually made an appearance in the studio whilst all of this was going on.

"Doing the instrumentals was a bit strange," recalled Simon Wright. "We had these TV screens which showed us the relevant parts of the movie, and we had to fit the music to the action."

The video to accompany 'Who Made Who' was a strange affair. Shot at the Brixton Academy in London and directed by the veteran David Mallet, let's leave the on-the-spot Mark Putterford to explain what was going on:

'It features footage of the band onstage surrounded by hordes of headbanging Angus lookalikes, as well as various shots of 'andsome Angus going through interesting, and at times quite funny, rockin' routines.

'The extras had been recruited through several sources: some from the band's fan club, some via Radio One and a lot more simply by word-of-mouth. It was a long, tiring and exacting day for them, but talking to the willing recruits between shots, it was clear that they had enjoyed their day out. They'd come from all over the country, but they went home happy... and with their specially supplied cardboard guitars autographed by Angus, Malcolm, Brian, Cliff and Simon.

'Backstage, the band were really enjoying themselves, despite the long waiting between scenes, spending their time watching videos (mainly 'Yes, Prime Minister' and 'The Comic Strip Presents'). Angus is the star of the video and had to endure the discomfort of being in a harness for most of the day, but the amusement of watching hundreds of replicas of himself was more than enough to keep him and the rest of the band occupied...'

On May 3, 'Who Made Who' was issued, becoming the band's biggest hit in years as it soared to Number 16. A month later, the album reached Number 11. *Kerrang!*'s Sylvie Simmons rated it highly – very highly!

'This AC/DC album, like just about any other AC/DC album you care to mention, is so skin-crawlingly sleazy you need a bottle of penicillin just to listen to it! Only difference is that two-thirds is familiar sleaze... Like 'You Shook Me All Night Long' and 'Hell's Bells', two of the good things I remember from 1980, and 'For Those About To Rock', 'Sink The Pink' and 'Shake Your Foundations', progressively more recent, but nonetheless stompingly fine, not forgetting Side

THE 'WHO MADE WHO'
LP SLEEVE, 1986

ANGUS (WITHOUT CAP) AND ASSORTED LOOKALIKES ON THE 'WHO MADE WHO' VIDEO SET

One's closing number, 'Ride On', the slowest, dirtiest, low-down Blues this side of ZZ...

'The three chunks of unfamiliarity are 'Who Made Who', 'D.T.' and 'Chase The Ace' – the first song in the classic AC/DC tradition. the others a couple of Angus/Malcolm-composed instrumentals, the former one big riff, like an extended instrumental break at a gig, the latter your basic 'Cocaine' riff rip-off, a real muscle-flexer...

'As a collection of songs this is great, and as a movie soundtrack it's got to be up there with the best...'

Energised by the success of the single and album, the band then shot a video for 'You Shook Me...' in June, again with David Mallet. This time they used a number of long-legged lovelies, with Page 3 model Corinne Russell very much to the fore. The result was titillating and hilarious. Yet, strangely, the single failed to make the expected impact, peaking at a muted Number 46.

As for the film (starring a young Emilio Estevez), it opened in the States during mid-July to a general critical and commercial thumbs-down. It would seem that Acca Dacca had been the only ones to emerge from the project with any credibility!

On the back of the film's appearance in the US, AC/DC again took to the road in July, supported by Queensrÿche. What was supposed to be a quick two-month jaunt, though, just kept being extended because of demand for tickets, and the fellas finally finished in November. What was strange was that the 'Who Made Who' album had been something of a flop, only reaching Number 33 in America!

Kerrang!'s Steffan Chirazi caught the band's show at the Cow Palace in San Francisco: 'AC/DC live are an experience that will leave the first-time watcher agog, the second-time watcher ecstatic and the 10th-time watcher merrily exchanging dandruff with approximately 18,942 other die-hards.

'The essential ingredient in AC/DC's arena aura is that element that is so lacking in these times of over-elaborate hypertechnics: simplicity. And before you leap up and fog off about a band on auto who play without feeling, you're reading the words of someone who feared that the amount of sweat from Angus could cause his electrocution...

'Their orgy of lights, drums, sound and guitars is so intense, so climactic, that one feels like an over-excited voyeur witnessing the ultimate act...'

But despite their return to a higher profile in the UK, AC/DC's popularity in the *Kerrang!* readers' poll still wasn't exactly impressive. They were voted fifth best band (Iron Maiden came out on top), Angus was sixth best guitarist (Number One was Steve Vai), AC/DC were ninth top live band (Iron Maiden were again out on top), 'Who

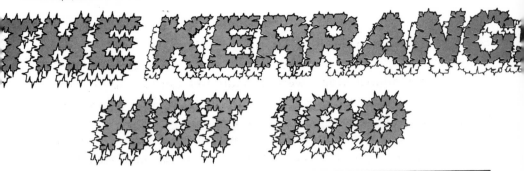

THE KERRANG! HOT 100

1 WHOLE LOTTA ROSIE **AC/DC**
2 STAIRWAY TO HEAVEN **Led Zeppelin**
3 STARGAZER **Rainbow**
4 PARANOID **Black Sabbath**
5 NUMBER OF THE BEAST **Iron Maiden**
6 RIME OF THE ANCIENT MARINER **Iron Maiden**
7 LET THERE BE ROCK **AC/DC**
8 SMOKE ON THE WATER **Deep Purple**
9 ANIMAL (F**K LIKE A BEAST) **W.A.S.P.**
10 CHILD IN TIME **Deep Purple**
11 2112 **Rush**
12 ACES HIGH **Iron Maiden**
13 FREEBIRD **Lynyrd Skynyrd**
14 BAT OUT OF HELL **Meat Loaf**
15 OUT IN THE FIELDS **Gary Moore & Phil Lynott**
16 ACE OF SPADES **Motörhead**
17 FORGOTTEN SONS **Marillion**
18 HALLOWED BE THY NAME **Iron Maiden**
19 PERFECT STRANGERS **Deep Purple**
20 FOR THOSE ABOUT TO ROCK **AC/DC**
21 KNOCKING AT YOUR BACK DOOR **Deep Purple**
22 STILL LOVING YOU **Scorpions**
23 RUN TO THE HILLS **Iron Maiden**
24 KAYLEIGH **Marillion**
25 THE TROOPER **Iron Maiden**
26 PHANTOM OF THE OPERA **Iron Maiden**
27 TOUCH TOO MUCH **AC/DC**
28 THE LAST IN LINE **Dio**
29 HOLY DIVER **Dio**
30 HEAVEN & HELL **Black Sabbath**
31 2 MINUTES TO MIDNIGHT **Iron Maiden**
32 HEARTLINE **Robin George**
33 GRENDEL **Marillion**
34 DOCTOR DOCTOR **UFO**
35 BARK AT THE MOON **Ozzy Osbourne**
36 LICK IT UP **Kiss**
37 HEAVEN'S ON FIRE **Kiss**
38 JUMP **Van Halen**
39 HELL'S BELLS **AC/DC**
40 KILLED BY DEATH **Motörhead**
41 CAROLINE **Status Quo**
42 CREEPING DEATH **Metallica**
43 EMPTY ROOMS **Gary Moore**
44 GIMME ALL YOUR LOVIN' **ZZ Top**
45 DETROIT ROCK CITY **Kiss**
46 ASSASSING **Marillion**
47 CRAZY TRAIN **Ozzy Osbourne**
48 ROCK YOU LIKE A HURRICANE **Scorpions**
49 HIGHWAY TO HELL **AC/DC**
50 DON'T TALK TO STRANGERS **Dio**
51 SCRIPT FOR A JESTER'S TEAR **Marillion**
52 WHOLE LOTTA LOVE **Led Zeppelin**
53 XANADU **Rush**
54 BOHEMIAN RHAPSODY **Queen**
55 POWERSLAVE **Iron Maiden**
56 BLACKOUT **Scorpions**
57 I WANNA ROCK **Twisted Sister**
58 HIGHWAY STAR **Deep Purple**
59 I SURRENDER **Rainbow**
60 SINCE YOU BEEN GONE **Rainbow**
61 SPIRIT OF RADIO **Rush**
62 747 (STRANGERS IN THE NIGHT) **Saxon**
63 HOT FOR TEACHER **Van Halen**
64 WHEELS OF STEEL **Saxon**
65 RAINBOW IN THE DARK **Dio**
66 GARDEN PARTY **Marillion**
67 PHOTOGRAPH **Def Leppard**
68 ALRIGHT NOW **Free**
69 ALL NIGHT LONG **Rainbow**
70 THE ZOO **Scorpions**
71 I AM (I'M ME) **Twisted Sister**
72 MR CROWLEY **Ozzy Osbourne**
73 CREATURES OF THE NIGHT **Kiss**
74 BALLS TO THE WALL **Accept**
75 SHOUT AT THE DEVIL **Mötley Crüe**
76 LEGS **ZZ Top**
77 SCHOOL DAZE **W.A.S.P.**
78 MOTÖRHEAD **Motörhead**
79 ROCK OF AGES **Def Leppard**
80 LAYLA **Derek And The Dominos**
81 RUNAWAY **Bon Jovi**
82 WISHING WELL **Free**
83 KASHMIR **Led Zeppelin**
84 AIN'T NO LOVE IN THE HEART OF THE CITY **Whitesnake**
85 SHARP-DRESSED MAN **ZZ Top**
86 ROCKIN' ALL OVER THE WORLD **Status Quo**
87 WE ROCK **Dio**
88 EGYPT (THE CHAINS ARE ON) **Dio**
89 FOOL FOR YOUR LOVIN' **Whitesnake**
90 NO-ONE LIKE YOU **Scorpions**
91 LOVE AIN'T NO STRANGER **Whitesnake**
92 DALLAS 1PM **Saxon**
93 ON A STORYTELLER'S NIGHT **Magnum**
94 PARISIENNE WALKWAYS **Gary Moore**
95 MARKET SQUARE HEROES **Marillion**
96 IN AND OUT OF LOVE **Bon Jovi**
97 BACK IN BLACK **AC/DC**
98 BLACK NIGHT **Deep Purple**
99 FAST AS A SHARK **Accept**
100 FUGAZI **Marillion**

AC/DC TOP THE *KERRANG!* READERS' HOT 100, 1985

Made Who' was only ninth top album (Maiden's 'Somewhere In Time' was first), whilst the single of the same name and the accompanying promotional video were seventh and fourth respectively in the top single and top promotional video sections (Bon Jovi's 'Livin' On A Prayer' won both). Not exactly a triumph!

However, AC/DC were doubtless far from bothered, as they took time out prior to regrouping in February 1987, ready once again to get on the treadmill...

CHAPTER FOURTEEN

THE ALL-ELECTRIC BLOW-JOB!

"I first heard AC/DC when I was at school. I just loved Bon Scott. To me, he was The Man, just amazing. I wish I'd been old enough to see him live. I was gutted when he died. I wonder how people would react to him today if he were still around? Probably call him crap! I do like Brian Johnson, though, and I'd still go to see the band whenever they play. You never know when it might be the last time!"
– Richie Glover (Dub War)

W hen AC/DC reconvened in Australia from their various homes scattered around the globe, Angus and Malcolm already had a pile of riffs on tape, worked out through a series of jams – as had been the case on every previous album.

To this, Brian Johnson added his own contributions, before the search was started for a suitable studio. Finally, they settled on Miraval in the South of France, and began the task of recording the new album during August.

"We looked at a number of different studios because we wanted a change, a bit of fresh air," Angus told Mark Putterford of *Kerrang!* in

October 1987. "Although the reason why this particular one was chosen has probably more to do with the fact that there's a golf course nearby and a few of the lads like to play golf! Either that, or the fact that they could go drinking in the clubs nearby."

The studio itself was a rustic, medieval-type construction with no air conditioning – which, considering the band were working in a climate known at that time of year for its hot weather, made for some uncomfortable nights! In fact, living conditions were so spartan that Brian and Cliff were forced to live in a shack attached to a local church.

"It was very basic. Mattresses on the floor. No air conditioning, and the bites we got from insects!" a laughing Johnson told *Kerrang!* writer Chris Welch. "But we had French women to cook us beautiful breakfasts. I couldn't stop eating. We had a ball!"

And back into the fold came both Harry Vanda and George Young, to act as producers on a full album for the first time in a number of years. Just like old times, then?

"We haven't worked with George and Harry in a long time," Angus told *Kerrang!*, "but we got back together to do the three new tracks on the 'Who Made Who' compilation album last year and we enjoyed it, y'know? It was fun. Plus, he's our brother, so there's no ego problems.

"When we first worked with George and Harry, they were mainly into doing commercial stuff, so they looked upon working with us as their pet; it wasn't all serious and arty-farty, it was just a chance to let their hair down and get stuck into some dirty rock 'n' roll.

"Also, George and Harry are honest enough to tell us if something is crap, and we don't mind them doing so if they're right. The difference between working with George and Harry and working with 'Mutt' Lange is that George and Harry are always looking for something different, whereas 'Mutt' is more interested in creating the perfect sound in the studio. 'Mutt' would worry about the sound of a pin dropping half-a-mile away, but George and Harry would rather look for something different musically – and that suits us, because we always try to come up with something different for each album."

The band actually ended up with no less than 19 songs for the new record...

AC/DC RECEIVE PLATINUM DISCS FOR AUSTRALIAN SALES OF 'BLOW UP YOUR VIDEO', 1988

"They're all great," explained Angus in October. "If it was up to me I'd put on all 19, but I reckon we'll have to settle for just nine or 10. We'll wait until they're all mixed before making up our minds which ones are gonna make it. There are gonna be a lot of goodies on the album, and a few surprises too - so watch out!

"Having said that, we're still as tough as ever – and there's definitely no BALLADS. I have a great aversion to slow songs. Apart from anything else, the world is saturated with the damn things... I don't mind hearing a ballad every now and then – like once a year, maybe – but even then I get pissed off after about two minutes. So whatever we try in the studio, it won't be a ballad!"

Pic Robert Ellis

INCREDIBLE AS it may seem, it's now over 21 months since AC/DC – the world's most irresistible rock'n'roll band – last thrust their perennially pleasurable powerchords onto the good people of Blighty.

Indeed, so vivid are memories of the **'Fly On The Wall'** shows – when the band proved night after night that they'd lost none of their fire, energy and uncanny ability to start every song like it was the first and finish it like it was the last! – that they could've happened a mere 21 *days* ago. Close your eyes and the vision of guitarist **Angus Young** pigeon-walking across the stage beneath a million coloured lights, picking out the intro to **'Sink The Pink'** is as clear as a Marquee lager.

Right now Angus is at home in Holland winding down by phone in the left...

■ **AC/DC** (ABOVE) have confirmed the following dates for their UK tour in March: Birmingham NEC March 8/9, Wembley Arena 11/12.

Tickets for all shows are priced at £10/£9, subject to a booking fee, which in the case of Wembley is 50p per ticket.

Tickets for the NEC are available now from the following outlets: NEC Box Office, Odeon and Ticket Shop (Birmingham), Cavendish Travel (Sheffield/Leeds), Piccadilly Records (Manchester), Goulds TV (Wolverhampton), Lotus Records (Stafford), Mike Lloyd Music (Hanley/Newcastle-Upon-Tyne), Way Ahead

(Nottingham/Derby), Town Hall Box Office (Leicester), Poster Centre (Coventry) and the Information Centre (Oxford).

Tickets for Wembley are available from: the Box Office, Tower Records (Piccadilly), LTB, Premier, Keith Prowse (credit cards are acceptable on: **01-741 8989**), Ticketmaster and Stargreen.

In addition, postal applications can be made for the Wembley dates via the following address: **Echo Box Office, PO Box 2, London W6 0LQ.** Please enclose a cheque/PO, made payable to **'MCP Ltd'**, and also an SAE. Please add on a 50p booking fee for each ticket.

with them is better for us."

. . . Better than working with **'Mutt' Lange**? I offer, detecting a slight tone of discontent in Angus' voice when he reflects on some of AC/DC's older albums . . .

"MUTT' IS great, you can't take anything away from the guy because he's so successful," says Angus, "and **'Back In Black'** was a good album. But that's because I think the songs themselves were great . . .

"The difference between working with George and Harry and working with 'Mutt' is that George and Harry are always looking for something different whereas Mutt is more interested in creating the perfect 'Mutt'..."

KERRANG! ANNOUNCE THE 'BLOW UP YOUR VIDEO' TOUR

As first info on the album – still untitled – was being announced, the band also revealed the dates for their '88 UK tour: Birmingham NEC March 8 and 9, and London's Wembley Arena 11 and 12. In fact, the band planned to spend virtually the whole of the year on the road. Within a few weeks, a third night at Wembley Arena had been confirmed for March 13. And at the beginning of 1988, the band burst back with a new single', 'Heatseeker', which quickly rose to Number 12 in the charts. And the album title, 'Blow Up Your Video', was also announced to the waiting public.

"We just went through that whole album with smiles on our faces," Brian Johnson told Chris Welch in *Kerrang!*. "The album is smashing, and we just knew it was going to be good. George has this father-figure approach, and he knows more about rock 'n' roll than any f**ker! Then you've got Malcolm and Angus there, so happy to work with their own brother and Harry too."

Johnson also revealed to *Kerrang!* that the album title came from a line in the chorus of one of the songs on the album ('That's The Way I Wanna Rock 'N' Roll').

"I suppose MTV will love it!" quipped 'Jonna', who went on to give *Kerrang!* a very brief guide to the forthcoming album:

" 'Heatseeker' will be one of the opening numbers on the tour. Another of my faves is 'That's The Way I Wanna Rock 'N' Roll', a great one for the stage. 'Mean Streak' has a great sense of humour. It's got a great driving beat. In fact, the whole album is UP. 'The Go Zone' is filthy, while 'Kissing Dynamite' is a cracker, I really like that one – a neck-bender to get 'em going. 'Nick Of Time' is very fast and 'Some Sin For Nuthin' ' is the only slow one, while 'Ruff Stuff' is another great stage number. 'Two's Up' is anything you want to think about, but the real cracker is 'This Means War'. It's so fast, we had to put it at the end. I'd say it's as fast as 'Riff Raff'."

The album was released at the end of January and reached Number Two in the UK charts – the best position since 'Back In Black'. In the US, meantime, it reached Number 12. Chris Welch was suitably ecstatic in the pages of the mighty *K!*.

'In an uncertain world, it is good to find that we can still be sure of the power of Rock. And more specifically, that power when it is unleashed by its most loyal and trustworthy exponents.

'No hair-tearing anguish over 'modernisation' here. No teams of keyboard players and computer programmers orchestrated by *wunderkind* producers. Just the brothers Young and their cohorts deftly delivering dynamic defiance.

'This is a package of songs played with almost spartan clarity. There's no clutter, no overloading the circuits, just a deep-seated conviction that all you have to do is bust a gut in the studio, just as you would do onstage. And that's the secret of this album's success. After you have sat through it and enjoyed each track, you feel like you've been to the Hammersmith Odeon... without the need to queue for hours for a plastic beaker of lager!'

The band began their lengthy sojourn back on the road in

Australia. Nothing unusual there, except that they hadn't actually toured back home since...

"The last time we were there was in 1981," said 'Jonna' to Welch, "and it was brilliant, it was a big thing for me. I met Bon's mother and father and his brothers. The tickets (for the latest tour) went on sale over there a couple of weeks ago, and in Sydney it was sold out in an hour, so they put on another show. When they put the tickets on sale in Perth, there were 63 arrests! They were fighting in the streets."

The tour itself proved to be sensational, stirring up interest from all quarters. And with Australia celebrating its Bicentenary as a nation, it seemed only fitting that their greatest ever Rock band should make a welcome return.

The tour kicked off at the Entertainment Centre in Perth on February 1. Bon's parents, Isa and Chick, were present in the audience – the first time they'd seen the band since their son had died. It all added to the atmosphere.

AC/DC eventually played two nights in Perth, four at the National Tennis Centre in Melbourne, three at the Entertainment Centre in Sydney, followed by one in Adelaide (the Globe Derby) and two in Brisbane (the Entertainment Centre).

Kerrang!'s Steve Mascord witnessed the triumphant homecoming in Sydney: 'The lights dim and disappear. A striking silver set – the equal of anything the American supergroups have come up with – is illuminated barely by fluorescent light as Brian Johnson, Malcolm Young, Cliff Williams and Simon Wright stride onstage in the near darkness. Angus Young emerges on the catwalk as 'Who Made Who' sets the sound and light into action.

'Then another Angus, and another, and another. 10 Angus Youngs – all winners of a lookalike contest – skip across the set and disappear before a strange green mist appears in the transparent tube that is the centrepiece of the AC/DC set. The real Angus rises from the tube and goes ape immediately as 'Who Made Who' gets into full swing. Seven years is a long wait and 13,000 Sydney-siders get close to drowning out their idols during the first number...

MALCOLM YOUNG ONSTAGE IN 1988

THE 'BLOW UP YOUR VIDEO'
ALBUM SLEEVE

'Brian Johnson tries to tell the crowd what the next song is, but all anybody understands from his thick Geordie accent is 'Back In Black' and 'Shoot T'Thrill'. Despite opening with Brian Johnson-era numbers, the show was strangely dominated by Bon Scott songs. A few from 'Back In Black', two from 'Blow Up Your Video' and the title tracks from 'For Those About To Rock...' and 'Who Made Who', and that was it as far as recent material goes.

'When this happened in Perth, many thought the presence of Scott's parents in the crowd was the reason. But it has continued, perhaps because in Australia Bon Scott *is* AC/DC. Just about every fan has a 'Bon Scott RIP' T-shirt and thinks of those early albums as definitive AC/DC music...

'Visually, the concert's magic moment came when, after a short break, the darkness was shattered by a breathtaking puff of smoke. The smoke clears, revealing a shirtless and horned Angus, who proceeds to play the unmistakable opening notes of Bon's anthem 'Highway To Hell'.

'The voice may sound a bit more gravelly, but Bon Scott lives again for the Aussies as AC/DC pump out 'Let There Be Rock', 'Whole Lotta Rosie', 'TNT', 'The Jack', 'High Voltage' and 'Dirty Deeds...'. As Johnson tore into 'For Those About To Rock', two giant cannons emerged from behind the set and let off their salvo to cue, to the immediate response and eternal deafness of the multitude... Afterwards, each band member was presented with a Platinum disc for Australian sales of 'Blow Up Your Video'... jeezuz boys, we salute you!'

After the monstrously successful return to Australia, the band headed to the UK and their series of arena dates. But with the band setting up shop in just two cities, surely they were guilty of

BACKSTAGE PASS FOR THE '88 WORLD TOUR

DOKKEN, AC/DC'S SUPPORT ACT FOR THEIR 1988 EUROPEAN TOUR

short-changing their British fans?

"A lot of fans in the North of England ask why they can't have the full show with all the effects like the Americans and Londoners," mused Johnson prior to the tour starting, when speaking to Chris Welch for *Kerrang!*. The problem is, they haven't got a building big enough up there. But we did play two nights at the NEC in Birmingham on our last tour and it was great, because we could put all the equipment up. We can just play as a band, without any cannons or bells, but it's much more enjoyable for the audience, the band and crew if we can put on the whole show."

It was an explanation anyhow, as to why AC/DC now stuck rigidly to the arena circuit – for better or for worse! With American foursome Dokken as their support act, the AC/DC 'Blow Up Your Video' show reached the UK.

'In recent years I have felt that AC/DC live are just becoming a one-man show,' wrote Dave Reynolds when reviewing one of the London dates for *Kerrang!*. 'Face it, apart from Brian Johnson's gravel-throated screaming, would you notice if Malcolm Young, Cliff Williams or Simon Wright were still in the band? They have hardly any stage presence at all, so Angus and Brian could quite easily appear onstage by themselves and you'd still get the same level of intensity every AC/DC performance has.

'What Wembley received tonight was a set, an intense set, packed full of old favourites. This was somewhat surprising, as I always thought the whole point of a tour was to encourage people to go out and buy the new album!

'Really, AC/DC could've played anything and the audience would've loved it. Angus is the people's hero, the Peter Pan of Heavy

1988 UK TOUR ADVERT

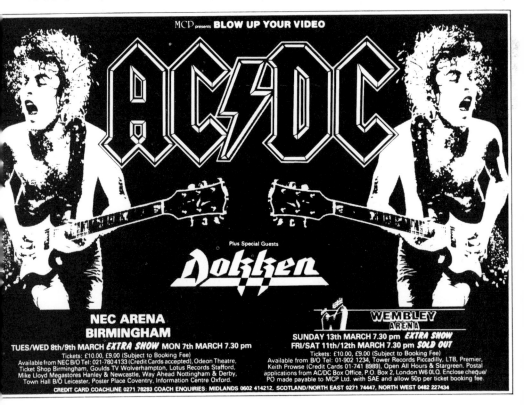

£1.32 Eire

No 169 · january 9, 1988 · 90p

KERRANG!

HAPPY NEW YEEARGH!

AC/DC BURST INTO '88

VIRUS INTRINSIC OVER KILL CRO MAGS GREAT WHITE

ANGUS YOUNG of AC/DC; pic George Bodnar

VOTE IN THE READERS' POLL

210

Metal. That boy ain't never gonna grow up now – he's trapped inside the schoolboy outfit forever.'

Reynolds went on to query the huge response from a predominantly male audience to Angus' strip-tease, and also bemoaned the fact that two fans were forcibly ejected and had 'the living daylights beaten out of them by at least four very big bouncers'. No, he didn't have the best of nights!

After the run at Wembley, the band headed out to Europe, before coming back to the UK to finish off this leg of the tour with a final date on April 13 at Wembley Arena. Then... America. But there was something sensational in the wind.

'AC/DC guitarist Malcolm Young will not be joining the band for their forthcoming US tour, due to the 'pressure of touring'.'

That was the simple announcement made in *Kerrang!* on May 7, 1988. This story went on to quote the official story from the band's management: 'Malcolm has always stressed that he plays with the band for the fun and enjoyment he gets out of it, and with the band having only just completed a hectic schedule of Australian and European shows, he felt that it was time to take a rest'.

Into his shoes stepped one Stevie Young, nephew of Angus and Malcolm and a member of Birmingham band The Starfighters, who had a sound very similar to that of Acca Dacca. Stevie made his debut with the band on May 3 as the band's US tour kicked off at the Cumberland Civic Centre in Portland, Maine.

The tour proved to be an enormous success for AC/DC. Stevie Young proved to be a worthy replacement for the temporarily absent Malcolm (his departure was never gonna be permanent). So much so that *Kerrang!* had this to say when the band played at the Meadowlands Arena in New Jersey: 'Some people have been saying that AC/DC are not the same without brother Malcolm in tow... Crap, the boys are still classic showmen.'

'Blow Up Your Video' proved to be the band's best-selling album in the States since 'For Those About To Rock...'. And when American troops used AC/DC's music in order to try and flush hated

THE FIRST *KERRANG!* COVER OF 1988

Panamanian dictator General Noriega out his embassy hiding place and into the arms of US justice, the band almost became overnight heroes and patriots!

Moreover, at a time when many major Rock bands were struggling to sell tickets in an American economy deep in the pockets of a recession, not only were Acca Dacca selling out everywhere, but they were being constantly forced to add more dates to their schedule – in the end, staying out on the road right up until December.

Meantime, back in Sydney Malcolm was slowly recovering from his problems, which turned out to be related to severe alcohol dependence and not just a case of 'exhaustion'.

"He's kicked his drink habit," Angus told Kerrang!'s Howard Johnson in September 1990, the first time that the real reasons behind Malcolm's departure were admitted. "He had to stop, it had just gone too far. From the age of 17, I don't think there was a day when he was sober. I suppose you could look at it as a record! I never knew how he could function like that. I don't drink, but everyone else was sure doing it for me!

"When the last album, 'Blow Up Your Video', came out he knew he had a problem. We toured Australia and the UK and he'd held up pretty good, he'd been doing his best. But after we finished here, he admitted that he wouldn't make it through America. We had about a week-and-a-half to decide what to do do between us, and we decided to ask my nephew Stevie.

"He did a great job. Most people thought it was Mal! They're very similar, he's got a strong personality. I was more nervous than he was."

Thus, Malcolm could spend time with his wife, Linda, and family back in Sydney, getting a semblance of normality back into his system. He even bought a race horse, in order to pursue an activity not related to music. However, he was also collating ideas for the band's next album. And when AC/DC finally came off the road in the States at the end of the year, he and Angus spent some time in London (at a house owned by Malcolm) and Holland (where Angus, of course, lived) working on basic riffs and melody lines.

ADVERT FOR THE 'HEATSEEKER' SINGLE AND UK TOUR, 1988

KONCERTZ
YOUNG AND CRAZY

AC/DC, DOKKEN
Wembley Arena

WEMBLEY IS a pretty shitty place to see your favourite bands, right? Stuck out on the edge of London it's unfortunately the closest thing the capital has to any of those American stadiums all the big bands play abroad. I hate it, so do a great many other people, including, it seems, Dokken.

After delivering a very disappointing set, opening up for everybody's favourite bunch of Aussies (well almost! I know the Young brothers are the only Australians left!) Don and the boys were spotted being very wild down at Hellion's Marquee show.

The last time Dokken were over here was, of course, in 1986, when they opened for Accept. I thought they were pretty good then but could sense the ill feeling on stage between Don Dokken and guitarist George Lynch.

Rumours abounded afterwards that Lynch was about to be replaced by former Holland axeman Mike Batio (now playing the LA clubs as Michel Angelo, having recently appeared on an album by self-proclaimed singing sensation Jim Gillete). Of course these were only rumours and Lynch is still a member of Dokken.

He doesn't appear to be a very ACTIVE member though, because for the majority of the set he chose to remain on the right side of the stage, seeming unaware that he had an audience at all. Lynch is a damn good guitarist, I just wish he'd get into the show a bit more rather than appear to be playing to himself.

The rhythm section of Jeff Pilson (bass) and 'Wild' Mick Brown (drums) were far more lively, but Dokken as a band still seemed to be operating at a low performance level, the mainman himself not being particularly outstanding out front.

I can't believe that they didn't really care about the performance because mention was made of technical problems, but it seemed funny how everything came together in terms of sound and presentation on 'In My Dreams', the band's encore which, quite frankly, they didn't deserve.

Don't get me wrong, I love this band, but I fear British fans will never see them at their best until they start headlining in this country. Something that's a long

THE ALL-ELECTRIC BLOW-JOB!

THE STARFIGHTERS (STEVIE YOUNG, SECOND RIGHT)

In the meantime, Cliff, Simon and Brian all repaired to different parts of the world in order to recuperate from their exertions. Stevie, meantime, headed back to Birmingham, having fulfilled his role to maximum effect. He now sought to put together his own band, Little Big Horn, but despite the backing of Part Rock Management and some positive press ('This band have the potential to be huge,' claimed Howard Johnson in *Kerrang!*), they achieved very little.

For Simon, though (who had moved out of London and to Fresno, California with his wife Desirée), this temporary separation from the band was about to become rather more permanent than he might have expected...

KERRANG! REVIEWED AC/DC AT WEMBLEY ARENA IN 1988

CHAPTER FIFTEEN

ON THE CUTTING EDGE

"AC/DC are one of the great rock 'n' roll bands of all time, and they'll never be eclipsed. I first heard them when my sister was getting into bands like The Police, and she handed me down 'Highway To Hell'. I listened to it and it blew my f**king head off! I said, 'This is the best shit I've ever heard!'. She said, 'You'll get sick of this soon'. But of course, that day never came!"

– Whitfield Crane (Ugly Kid Joe)

When work began on the material for the next AC/DC album in early 1989, rumours spread that Brian Johnson was on his way out of the band! What had happened was that Malcolm had cut some vocals on demos he and Angus had been working on, purely to give the pair an idea as to how the material was shaping up. Word, though, got out that this was being done by the Young brothers as a prelude to ousting their long-serving singer. Wrong!

The problem was that 'Jonna' was in the throes of getting divorced out in the States, and this was taking up most of his time. This was why he was unable to get heavily involved with the new stuff as it was being sorted out.

"Brian's been having a lot of personal problems, real shit," Angus told *Kerrang!*'s Howard Johnson. "Mal and I thought it would ease the pressure on him if we wrote the words... We've always contributed in

SIMON WRIGHT (SECOND RIGHT) WITH DIO
IN 1990

Wright lands job in Dio

■ AC/DC DRUMMER **Simon Wright** has parted company with the veteran Aussie Rockers and joined forces full time with **Dio**.

Wright originally hitched up with **Ronnie James** and co. just for the recording of their latest studio album, due in May through Phonogram.

The as yet untitled opus is currently being mixed in London by **Nigel Green**, who did the honours on **Def Leppard**'s blockbuster 'Hysteria'.

Among the tracks set for inclusion are 'Hey Angel', 'Evil On Queen Street', 'Born On The Sun' and 'Why Are They Watching Me'.

the past anyway. We'd sit down, all three of us, me, Mal and Bon – sometimes four of us with my brother George – and we'd have this big shoot-around. We always gave Bon a helping hand in the past; same with Brian, because if you have some lyrical idea while you're writing, it can save you a lot of heartache and trouble at the end of the day..."

Brian's position in the band was certainly safe. Which is more than can be said for Simon Wright...

Whilst Angus and Malcolm were busy working on material, Simon was approached by Ronnie Dio to play on the next Dio album 'Lock Up The Wolves'. This was meant to be merely a session situation for

Simon, to fill in time before AC/DC went back into the studio. However, it soon became a more permanent arrangement. And stories began to circulate that part of the reason, at least, for Simon finally opting to join Dio and jump ship from Acca Dacca was because he was being poorly paid! That did not amuse Angus when this was put to him by *Kerrang!*'s Howard Johnson:

"Well, he stayed long enough if he was being so badly paid! Financially, he couldn't expect to be paid the same as the members who had been there for years – but, hey, we all drank out of the same teacup.

"I don't think he felt he was a member, though! All the time I was around Simon, I only heard two words. They were 'Hello' at the start of the tour and 'Goodbye' at the end! I couldn't a word from him cos he was very quiet. He always felt like an outsider because we'd been doing it a lot longer than he had, so maybe that was our fault.

"But he always had a thing about Dio. When he first joined the band, he was always talking about Dio. He had a very close thing with Ronnie and I don't know why. He always spoke very highly of the guy. At the end of the day, I think he got bored sitting around waiting for me and Mal to get ready to go into the studio. He just got in touch one day and said, 'I'm off to do this Dio thing'...

"It was a bit stupid on his part, but he'd moved to America and was under some outside pressure."

Shortly after he made this decision, the author met Simon out in LA, as he was rehearsing with Dio. The drummer made it plain that, as far as he was concerned, the reasons for leaving were purely musical and had nothing to do with any personal or financial differences. Simon simply did not want to hang around, proverbially kicking his heels whilst the Youngs worked up songs for the new album.

However, the author *did* catch a sense of slight irritation from Simon as far as AC/DC were concerned. From the manner in which he spoke, there was plainly some personal friction between them, and hints were thrown out that he wasn't paid what was considered a fair salary considering the huge size of the band.

Wright did not last long with Dio. In fact, Dio did not last long, the band splitting up when Ronnie James Dio rejoined Black Sabbath. Since then Simon has been working with Rhino Bucket, whom many

AC/DC 1991 (FROM LEFT):
BRIAN JOHNSON, CLIFF
WILLIAMS, ANGUS
YOUNG, MALCOLM
YOUNG, CHRIS SLADE

'THE RAZORS EDGE'
LP, 1990

have dismissed over the years as no more than AC/DC clones!

Now without a drummer, AC/DC started rehearsals for the new album in a barn close to Brighton. They brought in Chris Slade on a purely temporary basis, at the suggestion of their management. Chris had previously worked with Gary Moore, who shared the same management as Acca Dacca.

Eyebrows were considerably raised at this choice. Slade, completely bald, was not the sort of person you'd expect to see involved with AC/DC. He'd been drumming since 1963 in a succession of bands. His first success came in 1965 when he played on the Tom Jones hit single 'It's Not Unusual'! Slade subsequently toured extensively with the Welsh warbler, before quitting in 1969 to join a group called Toomorrow *(sic)*, a flop act these days known for launching the career of one Olivia Newton-John!

The next port of call in Slade's chart career was Manfred Mann's Earth Band, whom he joined in 1972, working on three UK hit singles including the seminal 'Davy's On The Road Again'. That stint lasted seven years, after which Slade worked on an album with Scottish vocalist Frankie Miller, before joining Uriah Heep for their 1980 'Conquest' album and tour.

After that, the much sought-after Slade teamed up with Gary Numan, Bad Company guitarist Mick Ralphs (in the disastrous Mick Ralphs Band) and toured with Pink Floyd guitarist Dave Gilmour, prior to teaming up with Jimmy Page, Paul Rodgers and bassist Tony Franklin in the ill-fated supergroup The Firm. Two albums down the line, this quartet fell apart, and Slade joined up with Gary Moore on a

temporary basis, taking over from Cozy Powell. It was his intention after this to put together a band with ex-Aerosmith guitarist Rick Dufay. But the call from AC/DC scuppered those plans.

"I think Mal saw him playing with Gary Moore (in Los Angeles) and he said he was a good Rock drummer," Angus told Howard Johnson in *Kerrang!*. "So when Simon left, Chris' name came up. He sat in, we tried him out and he fitted in great.

BACKSTAGE PASS FOR 'THE RAZORS EDGE' TOUR

"He's another one who can bang 'em. He's like Phil (Rudd), a bit frightening, a big guy looming over the kit. When we did the album he was just helping out, because we didn't want a session drummer. You'd be better sitting with a drum machine if that was what you were after. Things worked out so well that we asked if he wanted to join, and he was into it."

The rehearsals for the album having gone exceptionally well, the new line-up left Brighton and headed for Windmill Road Studios in Ireland to start work in earnest on the new record. But this time, Vanda and Young were not to be involved. Instead, top Canadian producer Bruce Fairbairn was brought in.

"We were gonna use my brother George, but he had other commitments, so we were on the hunt looking for someone new," Angus explained to Johnson in *Kerrang!*. Exactly what these 'other commitments' were, nobody was divulging. Nor the reason why it was only to be George Young involved on the production side and not the Vanda and Young team. But back to Angus in *Kerrang!*:

"These days, I think it's pretty hard to find someone to produce you who's really into Rock music, so we asked around and the word came back that Bruce Fairbairn was the best.

"So my brother Mal went out to Vancouver to have a chat with the guy, shoot the breeze. Cos there was one thing that we were worried about, and that was the fact that people on the American side like to be very commercial, y'know, the Rock ballads and all that.

"But the first thing he said was that he wasn't there to change us. He was very smooth to work with. He just wanted us to be happy... I think it helped that we had everything written before we went in this time, so we weren't working changing this and changing that.

"On a business side, it wasn't tough to come to an arrangement (with Fairbairn). He was very keen to do it, cos he told us that in the past a lot of bands had come to him and asked for the AC/DC sound."

In the end, all of the recording was done at Fairbairn's own Little Mountain Studios in Vancouver, where he'd already worked his magic with Aerosmith and Bon Jovi in the recent past. The whole

ANGUS FOOLS AROUND IN 1990

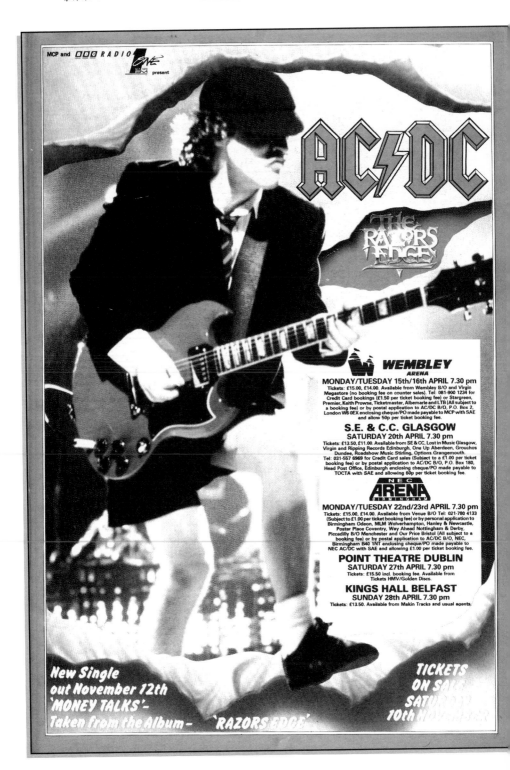

KING'S X, AC/DC'S EUROPEAN TOUR SUPPORT ACT IN 1991

process took just six weeks to complete. And Angus, for one, was very happy with the result, an album they titled 'The Razors Edge'. He told Johnson in the mighty *K!*:

"You always make the best album you can for that period. We never have, never would, put something out unless we felt confident about it. This time, we kept pushing the deadline (for completion) further and further back so that the record was right.

"In the past, we've already been committed to touring and there wasn't even a record ready! This was a good one, because when we finished touring in '88, Stuart (Young, co-manager) said we could have free rope to sit down, take our time to write the next record and not feel any pressure, which left me and Mal with a clear field to be able to sit down and write at leisure."

First release from the album was the single 'Thunderstruck', which rocketed up to Number 13 in the UK charts, backed up by yet another promotional video directed by David Mallet, which depicted rows

**AC/DC ONSTAGE IN 1991 - WITH THEIR INFAMOUS
'WHOLE LOTTA ROSIE' DOLL!**

of Acca Dacca fans headbanging their way through the number as the band went through their chops.

And in September, 'The Razors Edge' was unleashed by the band's new label Atco (they'd switched there from Atlantic after the last album concluded contractual obligations; EastWest, though, still marketed and distributed AC/DC's product) with a special launch party

held at the infamous School Dinners restaurant in London's West End – famed for waitresses who cavorted about in naughty schoolgirl attire. Presumably, the choice of venue was somewhat inspired by Angus!

The album proved to be a huge seller, reaching Number Four in the UK charts and getting up to Number Two in the US. Indeed, this record took Acca Dacca's total worldwide sales past 60 million copies – a staggering achievement. In addition, they also breached the Top 40 singles chart in Britain with 'Moneytalks' (complete with a live video shot in Philadelphia) and 'Are You Ready?' (the video for which saw a number of extras parading with the AC/DC logo shaved into the back of their heads!).

Two long-form video collections were also released during this period, namely 'Who Made Who' (which featured footage covering the years between 1980-86) and 'Clipped' (which brought together the promotional videos shot for both 'Blow Up Your Video' and 'The Razors Edge'). AC/DC were, commercially speaking, as strong as they'd ever been.

But, how did *Kerrang!* react to the new album? With certain reservations...

'With the possible exception of the title track to 'Who Made Who', nothing they have released in almost a decade now has managed to step out from beneath the imposing shadow of the band's long and illustrious past, to compare convincingly with recognised AC/DC classix...' claimed Mick Wall. 'Still incapable of delivering an essentially bad album, to succeed now on the scale they enjoyed 10 years ago, however, AC/DC must prove that they are still ready and able to deliver something exceptional.

'This, sad to say, 'The Razors Edge' singularly fails to do. It sees the whole concept of AC/DC showing its age badly. Even the practised and much in demand hand of producer Bruce Fairbairn cannot save the 'new' material from itself: mostly just average, sweaty exercises in professional water-treading... the plain fact of the matter is that the new shit ain't half as good as the old shit. I can't help wondering what Bon Scott would have made of the new AC/DC album. I imagine him laughing: "Pile of f★★king shit, mate!".'

In November, *Kerrang!* announced details of the band's planned UK tour in April '91: Wembley Arena April 15/16/17, Glasgow SE&CC 20, Birmingham NEC 22/23/24, Dublin Point Theatre 26 and Belfast King's Hall 27. Around the same, the band started yet another huge world tour back in the States. And *Kerrang!*'s East Coast correspondent Don Kaye was very impressed when he reviewed them at the Meadowlands Arena (supported by Love/Hate)...

'After 15 years (AC/DC are) playin' one muddafuggin' hot set, and even if there's two too many Angus guitar masturbation sequences and Brian Johnson doesn't quite hit all the notes, it was still givin' me goosebumps – even as the boys passed the two-hour mark... The bell rang, Angus rolled down ramps and catwalked across, er, catwalks, fake money fell from the sky during 'Moneytalks' and, of course, the cannons fired.

'And the set list? If you're unhappy with this one, just leave: 'Thunderstruck', 'Shoot T'Thrill', 'Back In Black', 'Fire Your Guns', 'Sin City', 'Heatseeker', 'Who Made Who', 'Jailbreak', 'The Jack', 'The Razors Edge', 'That's The Way I Wanna Rock 'N' Roll', 'Moneytalks', 'Hell's Bells', 'High Voltage', 'You Shook Me All Night Long', 'Dirty Deeds Done Dirt Cheap', 'Whole Lotta Rosie', 'Let There Be Rock', and the encores 'Highway To Hell', 'TNT' and 'For Those About To Rock'. 'Nuff said?'

'Nuff indeed. What with huge inflatable dolls, larger-than-ever cannons and a Godzilla-style approach to stage production, Acca Dacca were delivering performances that befitted their status as one of the all-time great Hard Rock acts. And they were selling out venues everywhere they went.

Tragedy, though, struck on January 18, when at the Salt Palace in Salt Lake City three fans (14-year-olds Jimmy Boyd and Curtis Child

ADVERT FOR THE 'MONEYTALKS' SINGLE, 1991

METALLICA, SECOND ON THE BILL AT DONINGTON '91

MÖTLEY CRÜE, THIRD ON THE BILL AT DONINGTON '91

QUEENSRŸCHE, FOURTH ON THE BILL AT DONINGTON '91

THE BLACK CROWES, OPENERS AT DONINGTON '91

LOOKIN' FOR STUBBLE

11 years ago, there were *two* cleanshaven youngsters with blazers and satchels in Manchester Apollo for the AC/DC show; one was the diminutive human dynamo ANGUS YOUNG, the other was the dimwitted subhuman dig-a-you HOWARD JOHNS Now, after all this time – and on the eve of the release of AC/DC's 13th studio albu Razor's Edge' – they finally meet. Hojo has started shaving and is out of short pan Angus is still wearing his but *still* doesn't look old enough to pick up a Bic Disposab

and 19-year-old Elizabeth Glausi) were crushed to death as the crowd surged towards the stage when the band's show began.

The band were especially upset by reporting at the time that suggested they 'callously' played on with complete disregard for the safety of fans.

In a statement to *Kerrang!*, AC/DC said: 'The events of this calamity occurred in a very quick time frame. Once the gravity of the situation was communicated to the band, they immediately stopped performing, but stayed onstage in an effort to minimise the confusion. During this time singer Brian Johnson made several requests with the audience to clear the area. AC/DC's management co-operated with the Salt Lake City Fire Marshall and other health and safety officials to maintain calm and order.

'After 15 minutes, the decision to finish the performance was made with the Fire Marshall. This decision was motivated in order to maintain calm and order among the thousands of fans who were unaware of what had occurred.'

"It was chaotic, it was hell," one eyewitness (Scott Neil, a friend of Child) told *Kerrang!*. "People were screaming. After they started another song, people started chanting, 'Stop the concert, stop the concert' until it echoed, but they wouldn't. When they started another song, I didn't think I was going to make it."

Another eyewitness, 39-year-old Gertrud Scheffler, told how one security guard had tried to get the band to stop playing when the crowd surged forward: "He was frantic, trying to get the lead singer's attention. He was making motions across his neck, like to cut. You could see he was desperate."

The band, though, were not to blame in the slightest for the incident, and suffered no lasting effect. But it was ironic that the last previous fatalities at a Rock concert in the States had occurred in 1979 outside the Cincinnati Riverfront Coliseum, when 11 people were killed as the crowd surged towards the doors. The Who were headlining that night. Their support band? AC/DC!

Putting this heart-rending disaster behind 'em, the Acca Dacca

ANGUS YOUNG INTERVIEW IN *KERRANG!*, 1990

machine rolled inexorably onward, reaching Europe on March 20, when they played in Helsinki. And, as the band prepared to hit the UK (supported by Texan trio King's X), they confirmed their previously-discussed record-breaking third headlining slot at Donington in August 1991.

Paul Elliott caught up with Acca Dacca in Mannheim, Germany at the start of their Euro '...Edge' trek. He fielded this report back to *Kerrang!*: 'The show was exactly what Rock fans all over the planet have come to expect from the original bad boys of Boogie: two hours plus of the hardest, no-frills rock 'n' roll. Give or take a couple of songs and a surprise or two, Donington should get what Mannheim got: the definitive AC/DC show. They play pretty much everything... Not many can follow AC/DC, the archetypal Monsters Of Rock'.

At Wembley, Xavier Russell was equally as convinced of the band's prowess: 'The new stage set-up is quite impressive, a mass of STEEL GIRDERS and WALKWAYS looking not dissimilar to the NEXT SHOP in (London's) Oxford Street. As the drumkit slowly emerged from beneath the stage, the familiar kry of "ANGUS! ANGUS!" slowly got louder and louder. When he appeared the krowd erupted...

'They opened rather prediktably with 'Thunderstruck', Angus kommanding the stage like he always does and 'Beano' Johnson koming akross like Harry H Corbett on SPEED with his kontinual runs bakk and forth – and new drummer Chris Slade seems to be quite a find with his hard skin-pounding.

'The legendary BELL makes its appearance during 'Hell's Bells' and the band finally go into overdrive on 'High Voltage'. It's strange how the whole band seem to go up a gear on the older material... everything played from the pre-'Back In Black' era sounded more FRESH and ENERGETIK. The energy level got to boiling point two hours five minutes into the show with enkore 'Highway To Hell', which kame komplete with an inflatable Angus head with glowing eyes!

'This was truly a remarkable display from a band who still get a

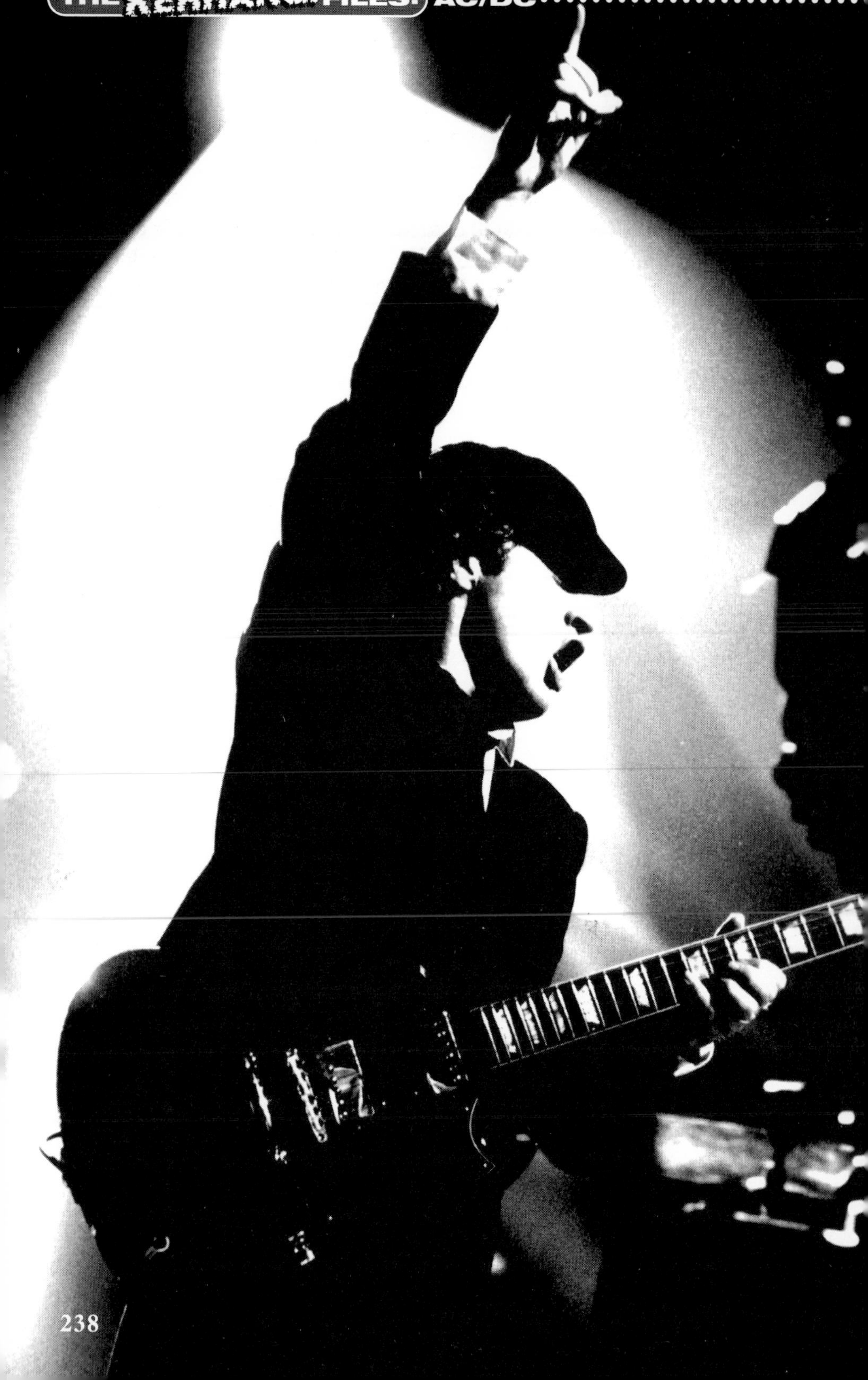

charge every time they tread the boards...'

The band headed back to the States after Europe, this time supported by LA Guns. They even took in some outdoor venues as the weather hotted up. And then it was back to Europe for Donington and a series of 20 Monsters Of Rock festivals across the continent in 18 cities. This included one free show at the Tushino Airfield in Moscow that attracted an estimated 500,000 fans to see Acca Dacca, Metallica, Pantera and the Black Crowes.

This last date celebrated the failure of the attempted Communist counter-coup in the Soviet Union and was to be the basis for a long-overdue event in 1992: a live album featuring Brian Johnson!...

CHAPTER SIXTEEN

GOING LIVE...
AND BEYOND!

"AC/DC are the best at what they do. It's as simple as that. I wouldn't say that I like everything they've done, but in their own way, they are as classic a band as Led Zeppelin or Deep Purple..."
– Tony Iommi (Black Sabbath)

"O h, sure there'll be another live album. We don't have any plans at the moment, but there will definitely be one in the future – because we haven't done anything with Brian yet. The main reason why we've waited so long is that we wanted to get enough new material under Brian's belt first, so he wouldn't have to sing old songs all the time. But now, we've got enough good material to choose from, so maybe we'll make some plans soon."

That's what Malcolm Young told *Kerrang!*'s Mark Putterford in January 1986. However, we were to wait a further five years before the band finally announced details of their second official live album. In October 1991, *Kerrang!* made the following announcement:

'Aussie Boogie giants AC/DC will release a double live album, as yet untitled, through Atlantic next year. The band have recorded several shows on their 'Razors Edge' world tour'.

"We did it for the hell of it," Brian Johnson told *Kerrang!*'s Murray Engleheart. "We said to each other, instead of going in and saying we'll do a live album, here, we'll just record it all over the world at different spots, and then get the tapes together. It will be great."

Among the shows recorded was the historic date in Moscow. And Donington was filmed by director David Mallet using no less than 22 cameras. It wasn't until September 1992 that the band finally broke

**THE SLEEVE FOR THE
'LIVE' ALBUM, 1992**

the full story on their impending live extravaganza in *Kerrang!*. The release date for the album, simply titled 'Live', was set for October 29. The production was handled by Bruce Fairbairn and featured a selection of tracks drawn from 153 shows on the 'Razors Edge' trek.

The album would be preceded by a single, 'Highway To Hell (Live)' on October 5. And in addition, the live video shot at Donington would be coming out before the end of the year, under the inspiring title of 'AC/DC Live At Donington'.

"Every kid I've ever met at our shows, the first thing they always ask is, 'When are we getting this live album you've been promising for 11 years?',," Angus told Paul Elliott when *Kerrang!* caught up with the guitarist in Cologne, just prior to the record and video hitting the streets. "Plus, Brian's been with us a long time and recorded a lotta strong stuff."

Angus also reminisced with Elliott about 'If You Want Blood...': "(It) was the magic show. One night, guitars outta tune, feedback, singer farting, whatever. The title came from a gig we did in America, the Day On The Green festival. 80,000 people turned up. We were on at 10.30 in the morning, and most of us hadn't even been to bed!

"This guy from a film crew got hold of me and Bon and asked what kind of a show it was gonna be. Bon said, 'You remember when the Christians went to the lions? Well, we're the Christians!'. Then he asked me and I said, 'If they want blood, they're gonna get it!'."

THE SLEEVE FOR 'LAST ACTION HERO', 1993

MUSIC FROM THE ORIGINAL MOTION PICTURE

LAST ACTION HERO

AC/DC
ALICE IN CHAINS
MEGADETH
QUEENSRŸCHE
DEF LEPPARD
ANTHRAX
AEROSMITH
CYPRESS HILL
FISHBONE
TESLA
MICHAEL KAMEN
WITH BUCKETHEAD

Angus also revealed to Elliott his feelings on playing live: "The shows go so quick. You're on and you're off and you have to go back to how you are as a person. That's the hard part, because once you go into being The Schoolboy, it's pretty hard to come off it. It's two different people... I've been up there playing and thinking, 'What are those feet doing?'! I'm watching 'em to see which way they wanna go! That's all I ever do, follow the feet and the guitar. The duckwalk came naturally. As a kid, I was never one for the Cliff Richard thing with the tennis racket. I was more interested in getting my fingers 'round the guitar neck."

Elliott was suitably impressed with the live LP when he reviewed it: 'AC/DC are still one of the greatest live bands on the planet, and the tracklisting on this heavyweight double live album is awesome... After 12 years, Brian's 40-a-day growl is as much a part of the AC/DC sound as was Bon's snotty, drunken hollering – although, as Angus admits, you can't but think of the leering old bastard when Brian slurs 'The Jack' or the downbeat parts in 'Jailbreak' and 'Sin City'...

' 'Live' is a document of the entire 1990-91 'Razors Edge' tour. It was recorded all over the world. The album's only failing is that the material from various gigs is separated – one crowd faded out and another faded in – thus losing the impetus that was so crucial to the energy and excitement of 'If You Want Blood...'. 'Live' is not the definitive AC/DC album – if there is such a thing, it's either 'Back In Black', 'Highway To Hell' or 'If You Want Blood...'. This is still a great live album, though. What else would you expect from AC/DC?'

As for the video, Chris Watts had this to say about it in *Kerrang!*: 'David Mallet's lavish, 22-camera extravaganza positively revels in the record-breaking attendance for AC/DC's third headlining show at Donington. If you're after a state-of-the-art, uninterrupted documentary of a gig, then this can hardly fail to satisfy. It is a massive display. AC/DC, after all, are probably one of the greatest live bands in Metal, and that in itself makes for some prime-time entertainment. But AC/DC are also one of the safest live bands in Metal. That makes this

DETAIL FROM THE PACKAGING OF THE 'LIVE' ALBUM, 1992

straight concert footage with a running time just four minutes shy of two hours into something of an endurance test for all except the absolutely fanatical...

'(However) with zero backstage or interview footage, 'AC/DC Live At Donington' is simply a pristine postcard from the big field. If that's all you require for your money, then vote with cash. You can't, as the actress said to the politician, go wrong.'

Sadly, the band elected not to tour on the back of this release, but rather to conserve their energies for the next bout of studio activity, which *Kerrang!* reported in early 1993 would be a back-to-basics effort. However, there was a flurry of activity during the Summer when Acca Dacca recorded a new song, 'Big Gun', for the soundtrack of the latest Arnold Schwarzenegger blockbuster 'Last Action Hero', the album for which was due for release through Columbia in July.

Also on the record were the likes of Alice In Chains, Megadeth, Def Leppard, Queensrÿche, Anthrax, Aerosmith and Fishbone.

'Big Gun' was produced by Rock Rubin, whom *Kerrang!* revealed was on the short-list of producers being considered by the band for their next studio outing. And the video for this number actually featured Schwarzenegger himself; he even donned a schoolboy uniform similar to that worn by Angus at the clip's climax!

'Big Gun' was put out as a single by Atlantic on June 28, with live versions of 'Back In Black' and 'For Those About To Rock...' (both recorded at the Moscow Monsters Of Rock show in '91) included on the four formats – both never previously made available.

So, what was 'Big Gun' like? 'It has a typically dry Rubin mix, complementing a classically simple AC/DC arrangement. No fuss, plenty of clout. 'Big Gun' is pure AC/DC... Rick Rubin would be a good choice of producer for the next AC/DC album,' hailed Paul Elliott in *Kerrang!*. His comments on Rubin would prove prophetic indeed.

Both 'Big Gun' and the 'Last Action Hero' soundtrack were huge commercial hits, which is more than can be said for the film. In the meantime, Acca Dacca themselves were getting the big screen treatment across the UK, with the 'Live At Donington' video being shown at cinemas during June and July, in a 'tour' sponsored by *Kerrang!* and Radio One.

In addition, a long-form video titled 'For Those About To Rock We Salute You' was put out. It was an 84-minute documentation of the historic Moscow show, featuring footage from all the bands on the bill: AC/DC, Metallica, the Black Crowes and Pantera. Despite their absence from the touring circuit, AC/DC's profile was higher than ever, in one way or another.

It was in July 1994 that Paul Rees reported in *Kerrang!* that the band were preparing material for the next album, whilst also considering who they would be hiring to produce the record. According to Rees, Rick Rubin was among the hot favourites to land the job, with Bruce Fairbairn the other likely option. At the time, a release in February or March of 1995 seem possible, but this was only conjecture.

However, there was no denying the fact that Atlantic were preparing to re-issue nine of the band's classic albums over the coming few months in digitally remastered form. The albums in question were 'High Voltage', 'Dirty Deeds Done Dirt Cheap', 'For Those About To Rock (We Salute You)' – all due out on July 18, 1994. Then came 'Highway To Hell' and 'Back In Black' on August 15, with 'Let There Be Rock', 'Powerage', 'If You Want Blood... You Got It' and 'Flick Of The Switch' following on September 19.

This batch of releases fitted into the modern trend at major labels of remastering classic albums for the CD generation. 'The best drug money can buy,' is the way Paul Elliott described this collection in *Kerrang!* – and no one could argue with that!

By October of '94, it had become clear that the band were actually in New York working on the new record with Rick Rubin in the hot seat. And for the bearded American Recordings supremo, it was virtually a dream come true.

"Most of the kids in my high school were into bands like Led Zeppelin, Yes and Pink Floyd, and I spent a lot of time hating those bands. Two bands grabbed me, Aerosmith and AC/DC," Rubin had told *Kerrang!*'s Steffan Chirazi in 1987. " 'DC were kicking with that great, huge guitar. I remember being impressed by all the things they tell you are wrong – volume, power, the simple riffs. And Bon Scott was just brilliant."

Rubin had always let it be known that, among his ambitions, was the desire to work one day with both the 'Smiths and Acca Dacca.

ARNOLD SCHWARZENEGGER IMPERSONATES ANGUS YOUNG IN THE 'BIG GUN' VIDEO, 1993

Now, he was getting the chance with Angus, Malcolm and the rest.

However, there was very little information coming out of the AC/DC camp, which has been the norm with them for the last decade. Thus, as 1995 dawned, there was still no official confirmation that Rubin was producing 'em. Nor on the fact that the band had relocated to LA from New York to continue work on the album. Nor, for that matter, on reports that Phil Rudd was back in the fold.

Wait a minute! Phil Rudd?! Yes, word reached *Kerrang!* during early January that the classic Acca Dacca skinsman had come out of his enforced retirement to rejoin his old mates.

'Strong reports from Los Angeles, where the Aussie Rock gods are now working on their new LP, say that 40-year-old Rudd is back in the band and that the two parties have patched up their differences,' claimed *Kerrang!*. 'AC/DC's management deny these stories, saying that Chris Slade is still in the band. On the surface, reports of Rudd's return would seem highly unlikely, as he left the band on far from amicable terms...'

Indeed, as this book went to press, there was still no confirmation from official quarters on the drumming position. Yet an increasing amount of indirect evidence pointed towards the veracity of this story.

A short time later, more rumours were stirred into the Acca Dacca pot, one that was already close to boiling point.

'AC/DC are the hot favourites to headline Donington this year – and it could be their last ever UK show!' claimed *Kerrang!* in February 1995. According to this report, Acca Dacca were at this time the 'preferred choice to top the bill for a record fourth time'. The logic behind this story lay in the fact that a number of top international acts had already ruled themselves out of contention for this prestigious spot, for one reason or another, leaving the Aussie superstars virtually unchallenged as the most obvious candidates. But what about this being their last-ever UK date?

'There are further reports,' ran the *Kerrang!* report, 'that AC/DC intend to make their Donington appearance part of a farewell world tour, with drummer Phil Rudd returning to the fold after a 13-year absence!'

And there was more. It was even being suggested in certain quarters that Angus was getting fed up with parading around like a schoolkid onstage and wanted to wear long trousers for the upcoming tour! It was even being whispered that the band had gone so far as to rehearse with him in *jeans*! Sacrilege!

Still the fairy tales kept on coming. AC/DC, in the coming weeks, were off, on, off and on again as far as the Donington bill was concerned. It was reported that Brian, fed up with the band, had threatened to quit – and was only persuaded back on the promise that this would indeed be the farewell and album and tour for the fivesome.

Still, Johnson didn't seem to mind being in LA, spending any time he had free from studio duties out in the Santa Monica suburbs of LA in a local English-style pub, holding court and generally sounding in fine fettle.

Naturally, though, there was no word whatosever from the AC/DC camp. Ever since Bon's tragic death, they've kept their own

October 10, 1992 £1.20

KERRANG!

FALL TO YOUR KNEES AND REPENT!... EVERY WEDNESDAY!

INSIDE!
DEF LEPPARD:
Joe Elliott's
tour diary!

WARRANT
IZZY STRADLIN
SUICIDAL
TENDENCIES
PANTERA

SKID ROW:
Rachel Bolan's in
psychotherapy!

MEET
METALLICA AND
SEE 'EM LIVE
FROM THE
SNAKEPIT!

AC/DC

LIVE ALBUM AND VIDEO
WORLD EXCLUSIVE!!!
**ANGUS YOUNG ON
BON, BRIAN AND
BOYS IN SHORTS!**

counsel on plans and actions; even the band's own management and record label are kept at arm's length until the band are fully ready to unveil the latest studio platter and touring plans.

As this book goes to press, we are still no nearer to finding out exactly what the band have in mind for the next couple of years. They are still locked into their LA studio with Rubin putting the finishing touches to the new album. And touring plans are also being kept under wraps.

So, is this the end of the road for one of Rock's greatest-ever bands? Will we be bidding a fond, affectionate farewell to 'em in the not too distant future? Who can tell? To quote a cliché, all good things most come to an end. And AC/DC will leave behind a legacy of timeless music, stunning live shows and a fund of legendary stories that is the envy of virtually everyone else who has been involved with Hard Rock during the past two decades.

Most of all, though, they will leave behind millions of fans across the globe whose lives have been enriched by the entertainment they have sampled – both on record and onstage. If this were a video, the fitting end would be a collage of images spanning AC/DC's whole career, merging into one another to the soundtrack of the seminal 'Ride On'. But as this is a book, let me just take you back to late February 1980. Bon Scott had just died. At The Bandwagon in Kingsbury, North West London, they held a special memorial night in his honour.

The Bandwagon at this time was the most famous Heavy Metal disco in the country. The place was packed. And when 'Touch Too Much' was played, the atmosphere was somehow lifted. There were smiles on faces, hitherto stained by the tears of an inestimable loss. Maybe that's the most precious legacy AC/DC will leave behind: the ability to somehow turn sorrow and grief into joy. Perhaps that's why no other band is recalled with such warmth and depth of feeling. It's called entertainment. It's called genius. It's called... hell, what does it matter what you call it? Thank God we've all seen and felt the passion and power of AC/DC!

AC/DC'S MOST RECENT *KERRANG!* COVER APPEARANCE, 1992

AC/DC

THE UK
DISCOGRAPHY

SEVEN-INCH SINGLES

'It's A Long Way To The Top (If You Wanna Rock 'N' Roll)'/'Can I Sit Next To You Girl?' (Atlantic K 10745) – 1976

'Jailbreak'/'Fling Thing' (Atlantic K 10805) – 1976

'High Voltage'/'Live Wire' (Atlantic K 10860) – 1976

'Dirty Deeds Done Dirt Cheap'/'Big Balls/'The Jack' (Atlantic K 10899) – 1977

'Let There Be Rock'/'Problem Child' (Atlantic K 11018) – 1977

'Girls Got Rhythm'/'Get It Hot' (Atlantic K 11406) – 1979

'Touch Too Much'/'Livewire (live)'/'Shot Down In Flames (live)' (Atlantic K 11435) – 1980

'Rock 'N' Roll Damnation'/'Sin City' (Atlantic K 11142) – 1980

'Whole Lotta Rosie (live)'/'Hell Ain't A Bad Place To Be (live)' (Atlantic K 11207) – 1980

'High Voltage (live)'/'Live Wire' (Atlantic HM 1) – 1980

'Dirty Deeds Done Dirt Cheap'/'Big Balls'/'The Jack' (Atlantic HM 2) – 1980

'It's A Long Way To The Top (If You Wanna Rock 'N' Roll)'/'Can I Sit Next To You Girl' (Atlantic HM 3) – 1980

'Whole Lotta Rosie (live)'/'Hell Ain't A Bad Place To Be (live)' (Atlantic HM 4) – 1980

'You Shook Me All Night Long'/'Have A Drink On Me' (Atlantic K 11600) – 1980

'Rock And Roll Ain't Noise Pollution'/'Hell's Bells' (Atlantic K 11630) – 1980

'Let's Get It Up'/'Back In Black (live)' (Atlantic K 11706) – 1982

'For Those About To Rock (We Salute You)'/'Let There Be Rock (live)' (Atlantic K 11721) – 1982

'Guns For Hire'/'Landslide' (Atlantic A 9774) – 1983

'Nervous Shakedown'/'Rock And Roll Ain't Noise Pollution' (Atlantic A 9651) – 1984

'Danger'/'Back In Business' (Atlantic A 9532) – 1985

'Shake Your Foundations'/'Stand Up' (Atlantic A 9474) – 1986

'Who Made Who'/'Guns For Hire (live)' (Atlantic A 9425) – 1986

'You Shook Me All Night Long'/'She's Got Balls (live)' (Atlantic A 9377) – 1986

'Heatseeker'/'Go Zone' (Atlantic A 9136) – 1987

'That's The Way I Wanna Rock 'N' Roll'/'Kissin' Dynamite' (Atlantic A 9098) – 1988

'Thunderstruck'/'Fire Your Guns' (Atlantic B 8907) – 1990

'Moneytalks'/'Mistress For Christmas' (Atco B 8886) – 1990

'Are You Ready'/'Got You By The Balls' (Atco B 8830) – 1991

SEVEN-INCH EP

'Girls Got Rhythm'/'If You Want Blood (You've Got It)'/'Hell Ain't A Bad Place To Be (live)'/'Rock 'N' Roll Damnation' (Atlantic K 11406E) – 1979

CASSETTE SINGLES

'Nervous Shakedown'/'Rock And Roll Ain't Noise Pollution (live)'/'Sin City (live)'/'This House Is On Fire (live)' (Atlantic A 9631C) – 1984

'Thunderstruck'/'Fire Your Guns' (Atco B 8907C) – 1990

'Moneytalks'/'Mistress For Christmas' (Atco B 8886C) – 1990

'Are You Ready'/'Got You By The Balls' (Atco B 8830) – 1991

12-INCH SINGLES

'Rock 'N' Roll Damnation'/'Sin City' (Atlantic K 11142T) – 1978

'Whole Lotta Rosie (live)'/'Hell Ain't A Bad Place To Be (live)' (Atlantic K 11207T) – 1978

'Rock And Roll Ain't Noise Pollution'/'Hell's Bells' (Atlantic K 11630T) – 1980

'Let's Get It Up'/'TNT (live)'/'Back In Black (live)' (Atlantic K 11706T) – 1982

'For Those About To Rock (We Salute You)'/'Let There Be Rock (live)' (Atlantic K 11721T) – 1982

'Nervous Shakedown'/'Rock And Roll Ain't Noise Pollution (live)'/'Sin City (live)'/'This